MW01034975

GOD *Still* SPEAKS

JOHN ECKHARDT

Charisma
HOUSE
A STRANG COMPANY

Most STRANG COMMUNICATIONS BOOK GROUP products are available at special quantity discounts for bulk purchase for sales promotions, premiums, fund-raising, and educational needs. For details, write Strang Communications Book Group, 600 Rinehart Road, Lake Mary, Florida 32746, or telephone (407) 333-0600.

GOD STILL SPEAKS by John Eckhardt
Published by Charisma House
A Strang Company
600 Rinehart Road
Lake Mary, Florida 32746
www.strangbookgroup.com

This book or parts thereof may not be reproduced in any form, stored in a retrieval system, or transmitted in any form by any means—electronic, mechanical, photocopy, recording, or otherwise—without prior written permission of the publisher, except as provided by United States of America copyright law.

Unless otherwise noted, all Scripture quotations are from the King James Version of the Bible.

Scripture quotations marked NKJV are from the New King James Version of the Bible. Copyright © 1979, 1980, 1982 by Thomas Nelson, Inc., publishers. Used by permission.

Scripture quotations marked PHILLIPS are from The New Testament in Modern English, Revised Edition. Copyright © 1958, 1960, 1972 by J.B. Phillips. Macmillan Publishing Co. Used by permission.

Design Director: Bill Johnson
Cover design by Amanda Potter and Bill Johnson

Copyright © 2009 by John Eckhardt
All rights reserved

Library of Congress Cataloging-in-Publication Data

Eckhardt, John, 1957-
  God still speaks / John Eckhardt.
      p. cm.
  Includes bibliographical references
  ISBN 978-1-59979-475-4
  1. Prophecy--Christianity. I. Title.

  BR115.P8E34 2009
  234'.13--dc22

                                    2009009059

This publication is translated in Spanish under the title *Todavía Dios habla*, copyright © 2009 by John Eckhardt, published by Casa Creación, a Strang Company. All rights reserved.

10 11 12 13 14 — 11 10 9 8 7 6 5
Printed in Canada

CONTENTS

chapter one

THE HOLY SPIRIT AND A PROPHETIC CULTURE

FOR MANY YEARS, I have taught our congregation on the subject of prophecy, and I have seen the result of this teaching as thousands of people have been blessed and have learned to hear and move in prophecy. This is not theory to me, but rather, it is a lifestyle. I cannot imagine my life without prophecy. This is why this book is in your hands. I want to encourage you to become a part of a worldwide movement that is blessing countless lives.

It is important that we remain scriptural in everything we do. The Word of God provides safety and protection from misuse and abuse of prophecy. This book is filled with scriptural references on the prophetic life, and I encourage you to meditate on these verses. God wants to use His Word of truth to make your way prosperous and to cause good success. In each generation, God wants to develop a prophetic culture:

Behold, the days come, saith the LORD, that I will make a new covenant with the house of Israel, and with the house of Judah: not according to the covenant that I made with their fathers in the day that I took them by the hand to bring them out of the land of Egypt; which my covenant they brake, although I was an husband unto them, saith the LORD: but this shall be the covenant that I will make with the house of Israel; After those days, saith the LORD, I will put my law in their inward parts, and write it in their hearts; and will be their God, and they shall be my people. And they shall teach no more every man his neighbor, and every man his brother, saying, Know the LORD: for they shall all know me, from the least of them unto the greatest of them, saith the LORD; for I will forgive their iniquity, and I will remember their sin no more.

—JEREMIAH 31:31–34

It is clear that the new covenant God established with Israel and Judah includes knowing the Lord. All believers, from the least of us to the greatest, can have the blessing of knowing God through the Holy Spirit. This includes knowing and recognizing the voice of the Lord. When we use the term *prophecy*, we are simply referring to hearing the voice of the Lord and speaking His word to others.

In other words, every believer has the opportunity to operate in the prophetic realm. Every believer should expect to hear the voice of God. This is because each of us is a new covenant believer. The foundation of the new covenant is the basis for developing your prophetic life.

Every believer should expect to speak as the oracle of God. The key is to develop this ability intentionally. It will not happen automatically. Some believers have doubts about whether God will speak to them. Others can hear His word, but they struggle with speaking out on the behalf of God. All of us need more faith in order to flow in prophecy. Each of us must believe what the Word of God says and then act on it.

It is true: God wants every single person to be a prophet. Remember what Moses said:

> And Moses said unto him, Enviest thou for my sake? would God that all the LORD's people were prophets, and that the LORD would put his spirit upon them!
> —NUMBERS 11:29

This should be the heart of every leader. Moses desired that all of God's people would share in the prophetic anointing through the Holy Spirit being upon them. This is now a reality under the new covenant. We can all have the Holy Spirit upon us, and we can all share in the prophetic anointing.

Paul exhorted the Thessalonian church with these words:

> Therefore, brethren, stand fast, and hold the traditions which ye have been taught, whether by word, or our epistle.
> —2 THESSALONIANS 2:15

What traditions had the people of the Thessalonian church learned? What traditions have you learned over the course of your Christian life? Traditions include ideas, customs, skills, and tastes of a group of people that are transferred, or passed along, to succeeding generations. The customs of a people are the traditions they practice and transmit to future generations. There are some traditions that can keep people from obeying the Word of God. But

Jesus condemned the tradition of the Jews that made the Word of God of no effect.

There are, however, good traditions that bring order and blessing to society and to further generations. These traditions should be kept and maintained. Every church has traditions that have been passed down from previous generations. Some traditions need to be discarded, and some need to be kept and taught to succeeding generations. A change in tradition will cause a change in the culture of a church. Each church has a culture. Churches have a way of doing things that are transferred to succeeding generations.

This book is about developing a *prophetic culture* in the life of your church. The prophetic ministry is more than giving people "the word of the Lord" once in a while. In the context of a prophetic culture, the prophetic ministry will affect every area of the life of the local church. The prophetic ministry will affect the way people in a church live and operate.

Every believer should expect to hear the voice of God.

To *develop* means to build up or expand, to make stronger or more effective, to bring something that is latent into activity. The prophetic ministry is latent or dormant in the lives of many individuals and many churches, and as a result, there is a great need for activation. I want to help you develop in the area of prophecy. I want to stir your faith, and I want to impart the necessary knowledge you need to develop prophetically.

THE HOLY SPIRIT AND PROPHECY

Jesus promised His disciples the gift of the Holy Spirit. His promise was fulfilled on the Day of Pentecost—and in subsequent "pentecosts" over the centuries.

> And they were all filled with the Holy Ghost, and began to speak with other tongues, as the Spirit gave them utterance.
>
> —ACTS 2:4

The Holy Spirit is also known as the Comforter, and prophecy is one of the ways He comforts the believer. *Comforter* is the Greek word *parakletos*, which means an intercessor, consoler, or advocate. When the Holy Spirit comes, the results include comfort and strength and the ability to speak forth the word of God boldly.

The Holy Spirit "gave the disciples utterance," which in Greek is the word *apophtheggomai*, meaning to enunciate plainly, declare, say, or speak forth. The first thing that happened when the Holy Spirit came upon the disciples in the Upper Room on the Day of Pentecost was inspired utterance, which is prophecy.

In other words, the baptism of the Holy Spirit is the doorway into the prophetic realm. The well-known prophecy of Joel emphasizes the release of prophecy among the sons, daughters, servants, and handmaidens. The believers spoke with tongues on the Day of Pentecost, and Peter quoted the prophecy of Joel to identify what was happening. Those who spoke in tongues were inspired by the Holy Spirit:

> And it shall come to pass afterward, that I will pour out my spirit upon all flesh; and your sons and your daughters shall prophesy, your old men shall dream dreams, your

young men shall see visions: and also upon the servants and upon the handmaids in those days will I pour out my spirit.

—JOEL 2:28–29

Millions of believers worldwide have experienced the baptism of the Holy Spirit with the evidence of speaking in tongues. Many believers have limited their experience to speaking in tongues and have not experienced the blessing of prophecy. The believers in the New Testament church were able to speak in tongues *and* prophesy.

Both prophecy and speaking in tongues are forms of inspired utterance. It is easy to explain: speaking in tongues is inspired utterance in a language that is unknown to the speaker, and prophecy is an inspired utterance in a language that is known to the speaker.

The power of words

In order to fully understand the power of prophecy, we need a revelation about the power of the tongue. Jesus said that the words He spoke were spirit and life. Words—especially the words that come from God—are like spiritual containers that carry spirit and life.

The prophetic ministry is more than giving people "the word of the Lord" once in a while.

Words have power for both godly purposes and ungodly purposes. The entire universe came into being through words: "And God said, Let there be light: and there was light" (Gen. 1:3). Words can be used to bless or to curse: "Death and life are in the power of the tongue" (Prov. 18:21).

The Scriptures are filled with verses that emphasize the power of words and the tongue:

> He who speaks truth declares righteousness, but a false witness, deceit. There is one who speaks like the piercings of a sword, but the tongue of the wise promotes health.
>
> —Proverbs 12:17–18, NKJV

> Heaviness in the heart of man maketh it stoop: but a good word maketh it glad.
>
> —Proverbs 12:25

> A wholesome tongue is a tree of life: but perverseness therein is a breach in the spirit.
>
> —Proverbs 15:4

> A man hath joy by the answer of his mouth: and a word spoken in due season, how good is it!
>
> —Proverbs 15:23

> Pleasant words are like a honeycomb, sweetness to the soul and health to the bones.
>
> —Proverbs 16:24, NKJV

> A word fitly spoken is like apples of gold in pictures of silver.
>
> —Proverbs 25:11

> …a soft tongue breaketh the bone.
>
> —Proverbs 25:15

> How forcible are right words!
>
> —Job 6:25

Right words are forcible. The right word spoken at the right time carries tremendous power and force.

Words cannot exist without speakers, and speakers use their tongues in order to speak. Therefore, the Scriptures emphasize the power of the tongue for good as well as for ill:

> Even so the tongue is a little member, and boasteth great things. Behold, how great a matter a little fire kindleth! And the tongue is a fire, a world of iniquity: so is the tongue among our members, that it defileth the whole body, and setteth on fire the course of nature; and it is set on fire of hell.
>
> For every kind of beasts, and of birds, and of serpents, and of things in the sea, is tamed, and hath been tamed of mankind: but the tongue can no man tame; it is an unruly evil, full of deadly poison.
>
> Therewith bless we God, even the Father; and therewith curse we men, which are made after the similitude of God. Out of the same mouth proceedeth blessing and cursing. My brethren, these things ought not so to be. Doth a fountain send forth at the same place sweet water and bitter? Can the fig tree, my brethren, bear olive berries? either a vine, figs? so can no fountain both yield salt water and fresh.
>
> —JAMES 3:5–12

If words are this powerful, just imagine the power of inspired words! Words anointed and charged by the Holy Spirit carry tremendous power. A prophetic word can change your life. Prophecy is powerful because it is the word of the Lord, and no word from God is without power.

But there is a spirit in man: and the inspiration of the
Almighty giveth them understanding.

—Job 32:8

The inspiration of the Holy Spirit

God inspires our spirits through the Holy Spirit. The Old Testament prophets spoke by His inspiration. The New Testament prophets spoke by His inspiration. Spirit-filled believers today can also speak by the inspiration of the Holy Spirit.

The baptism of the Holy Spirit is the doorway into the prophetic realm.

Those who experience the manifestation of tongues can also prophesy. The Holy Spirit will inspire the believer to do both. The key is yielding to the Holy Spirit and allowing Him to inspire you to speak not only in a tongue that you do not comprehend and have not learned but also in your native language.

We believers can also pray by the inspiration of the Spirit. We can sing by inspiration. We can teach and preach by His inspiration. All results of the Holy Spirit's inspiration are different types of prophetic manifestations in action. We should welcome and cultivate all forms of the Spirit's inspiration.

In the New Testament, we are told not to stop inspired utterances: "Quench not the Spirit. Despise not prophesyings" (1 Thess. 5:19–20). Inspired utterances bring great blessing to the church and to individual believers. There is a tendency to stop or stifle inspired utterances in the church, and this is the reason Paul gave this admonition. When inspired utterances are stifled, the Holy Spirit is not at liberty to act. The Holy Spirit will inspire a person, but He will not force someone to speak. People can decide whether or not to utter an inspired message.

I have been inspired to prophesy to thousands of believers worldwide. I have seen the blessing of inspired utterance, and so can you. Yielding to the Holy Spirit's inspiration will bring countless blessing to those who hear your anointed words.

Words drop like rain

We read this line in a familiar psalm:

> The earth shook, the heavens also dropped at the presence of God....
>
> —PSALM 68:8

The heavens "drop" at the presence of God. What does that mean? *Drop* is the Hebrew word *nataph*, meaning to ooze, to distill gradually, to fall in drops, to speak by inspiration—in other words, to prophesy.

One of the ways God inspires us is by dropping His word upon us. This usually happens during corporate worship when the presence of God is strong. The word of the Lord falls like rain, and there are usually many in the service who get inspired to speak. Some will be inspired to sing prophetically as God drops a song upon them.

Words bubble up

Naba is the Hebrew word for *prophecy*, which means to speak or sing by inspiration (in prediction or simple discourse). The word carries the sense of bubbling or springing up, flowing, pouring out, gushing forth. The word for *prophet* is *nabiy*, which means an inspired man. The word for *prophetess* is *nabiyah*, which means an inspired woman, poetess, or prophet's wife. In other words, both men and women can be inspired to flow or bubble up with the words of God in prophetic utterances. The inspiration to prophesy can fall upon us like rain (*nataph*) or bubble up from the inside (*naba*). It is the same Holy Spirit who inspires in both ways, and the result is also the same—inspiration to speak forth the word of the Lord.

ENRICHED IN ALL UTTERANCE

The Corinthian church was "enriched in all utterance":

> That in every thing ye are enriched by him, in all utterance, and in all knowledge.
> —1 CORINTHIANS 1:5

The Holy Spirit will enrich each one of us in all utterance. When somebody or something has been "enriched," it has had something extra added to it. The word carries the idea of wealth or abundance. Because we have been filled with the Holy Spirit, we should abound in utterance. The Holy Spirit is a free Spirit (Ps. 51:12), which means He is liberal, generous, and magnanimous (willing to share Himself with us). He pours Himself out upon us, and His life flows out from within us. Most often, the outpouring of the Holy Spirit is released in an outpouring of prophecy. That is why we are urged not to quench or limit the Holy Spirit by quenching His inspiration.

The Holy Spirit will inspire a person, but He will not force someone to speak.

Inspired utterances are anointed by the Holy Spirit. These words carry tremendous power and authority. Anointed words can bring deliverance, healing, strength, comfort, refreshing, wisdom, and direction.

Inspired utterance has always been a key to breakthrough. It is interesting that the word *nathan* is translated "utter" in Scripture passages such as Joel 2:11 and 3:16, and Psalm 46:6.

> And the LORD shall *utter* his voice before his army: for his camp is very great: for he is strong that executeth his word.
>
> —JOEL 2:11, emphasis added

> The LORD also shall roar out of Zion, and *utter* his voice from Jerusalem.
>
> —JOEL 3:16, emphasis added

> The heathen raged, the kingdoms were moved: he *uttered* his voice, the earth melted.
>
> —PSALM 46:6, emphasis added

It is also interesting that Nathan is the name of the prophet who rebuked David after he slept with Bathsheba (2 Sam. 12). Once again, inspired utterance provided the key to the locked door of a human heart. In this case, the Holy Spirit inspired the prophet Nathan to tell a parable.

The earth melts when God utters His voice. This means the physical realm is affected by the voice of the Lord, and the physical realm includes men and women, not only because they dwell upon the earth but also because they were taken from the earth at Creation.

Inspired utterances have a dramatic effect upon men and women. Their lives are enriched through the prophetic words that are spoken. Mere human words could not achieve such results. Inspired utterances are not the work of a man but the work of the Holy Spirit.

The Holy Spirit speaks through us, and He puts His word in our mouths.

The Spirit of the Lord spake by me, and his word was in
my tongue.

—2 Samuel 23:2

David understood that his utterances were divinely inspired. David
would even sing under inspiration while he played on his harp. With
His word on your tongue, your tongue can become an instrument of
the divine. God desires to release His word by means of your tongue
and mine. He has given every believer the gift of the Holy Spirit to
accomplish His will.

Prophecy is the result of being filled with the Holy Ghost. Zacharias was dumb and unable to speak until his tongue was loosed
through the infilling of the Holy Spirit. Then he not only spoke some
words for the first time in months, but he also prophesied:

And his father Zacharias was filled with the Holy Ghost,
and prophesied, saying…

—Luke 1:67

Spirit-filled believers and churches *should* prophesy. By virtue
of being filled up with the Holy Spirit, we should overflow. *Filled*
is the Greek word *pietho*, meaning to imbue, influence, or supply.
Spirit-filled believers should speak by the influence of the Holy Spirit
because they have been imbued, influenced, and supplied with an
abundance of the life of the Spirit of God.

Under the influence of the Holy Spirit, we utter words that bring
edification, exhortation, and comfort, and there is always an abun-
dant supply of such utterance given to us by the Holy Spirit.

When someone is drunk, we say he or she is "under the influence." God wants us to be under the influence of His Spirit day in

and day out, and He expects that we will prefer His influence to that of alcoholic beverages:

> And be not drunk with wine, wherein is excess; but be filled with the Spirit; speaking to yourselves in psalms and hymns and spiritual songs, singing and making melody in your heart to the Lord.
>
> —Ephesians 5:18–19

As we live and operate under the influence of the Holy Spirit instead of being drunk or under the influence of wine, we will speak to one another and sing to one another divinely inspired words that inspire hope, joy, love, and thanksgiving.

A Prophetic Lifestyle

Under the old covenant, the Spirit of the Lord would come upon certain individuals and they would speak by inspiration. Sometimes we use the word *oracle* in connection with them. Today, every believer partakes of the Holy Spirit under the new covenant. We all have the Spirit within us, and we can enjoy the Spirit upon us because God has fulfilled His promise to pour out His Spirit upon all flesh.

Therefore, we can speak as the oracles of God:

> If any man speak, let him speak as the oracles of God.
>
> —1 Peter 4:11

Oracle is the Greek word *logion*, which means a brief utterance of God. God wants you to be His oracle. This is challenging to many believers who do not feel qualified to speak on behalf of God, but if you are one of them, you need to know that God has qualified you by giving you His Spirit. This is the blessing of the new covenant, and it is part of your inheritance as a believer.

I am attempting to simplify prophecy. There are different levels of the prophetic gift and lifestyle, but the most basic definition is speaking by the inspiration or influence of the Holy Spirit. We should not make prophecy more difficult than it is. Any believer can speak by the inspiration of the Holy Ghost, including you. As you walk into your full inheritance in the Spirit, you can do your part to build a prophetic culture in the body of Christ. It is a culture in which inspired utterances—in all their many manifestations—both bubble up and drop like rain wherever you may go.

chapter two

THE ROLE OF
PROPHETS TODAY

I AM NOT TRYING to make every believer a prophet. And yet all of us can prophesy. There are different levels of prophecy. An understanding of the different levels of prophecy will eliminate any confusion.

On the simplest level, a prophet is one who speaks words from God that build people up:

> He that prophesieth speaketh unto men to edification, and exhortation, and comfort.
> —1 CORINTHIANS 14:3

This is the simplest scriptural definition of *prophecy*. Prophetic words edify; they bring edification. To *edify* means to build up. God desires to "build up" His people through prophecy.

The word *edify* is related to the word *edifice*, which is another word for "a building." The church is God's building. His building (His edifice) is built up through prophecy.

How do prophetic words build up the church? By bringing exhortation and comfort to the individual people who make up the church. *Exhortation* is the Greek word *paraklesis*, which means solace, entreaty, consolation, admonition, or comfort. This word is related to the word *parakletos*, or Comforter, a name for the Holy Spirit. The Holy Spirit uses prophecy to comfort believers and to exhort them to holiness, love, worship, praise, prayer, evangelism, humility, and giving.

Comfort is the Greek noun *paramuthia*, which means consolation. This is a different type of comfort, and it is especially important for believers who are suffering or struggling in their faith.

It is important to note that this simple definition of prophecy contains no reference to prediction. This is where many people have erred, believing that *prophecy* is another word for predicting the future. While it is quite possible for prophets to offer prediction when they prophesy, it is not required by definition. Basic prophetic words adhere to the parameters of "edification, exhortation, and comfort."

PROPHETIC LEVELS

In the rest of this chapter, we will be exploring the various levels of prophetic utterance. You will begin to be able to see more options for channeling the flow of your own prophetic inspirations.

Spirit of prophecy

The most basic level of prophecy is known as the spirit of prophecy. As we worship God in spirit and in truth, the spirit of prophecy will manifest in our midst, and any believer can yield to this spirit of prophecy, speaking the word of the Lord.

The Lord wants to raise up a prophetic people (Num. 11:29), and the Holy Spirit is a prophetic Spirit (Acts 2:14–18). Therefore, the spirit of prophecy causes both men and women, sons and daughters, "servants and handmaidens" to prophesy. It provides people with the unction they need in order to speak as the oracles of the Lord, to use the biblical term.

We prophesy according to the proportion of our faith (Rom. 12:6). Our testimony is expressed prophetically:

> And I fell at his feet to worship him. And he said unto me, See thou do it not: I am thy fellowservant, and of thy brethren that have the testimony of Jesus: worship God: for the testimony of Jesus is the spirit of prophecy.
> —REVELATION 19:10

If believers act in faith when the spirit of prophecy is present, they all can prophesy. This does not make each one of them a prophet. Their utterances will be limited to the "testimony of Jesus." They will be speaking forth words of truth, valuable words of truth that are based on the revealed Word of truth in the Bible.

Basic prophetic words adhere to the parameters of "edification, exhortation, and comfort."

The Word of God testifies of Jesus. The more a person meditates on and knows the Word of God, the easier it will be to prophesy. The Word of God carries with it the spirit of prophecy. Then, as we worship God, the Word of the Lord can more easily bubble up in us or fall upon us, and we can prophesy freely.

The gift of prophecy

The second level of the prophetic realm is the gift of prophecy (1 Cor. 12:10). This gift can be stirred up:

> Therefore I remind you to stir up the gift of God which is
> in you through the laying on of my hands.
>
> —2 TIMOTHY 1:6, NKJV

Or a believer can yield to the spirit of prophecy and speak out of the additional strength of this gift as well. The utterances will be stronger than speaking by the spirit of prophecy only, because the person is speaking out of a gift.

There are levels of strength of the gift, depending upon the measure of grace received by the person who has the gift. Those who prophesy out of this level will speak words that will bring edification, exhortation, and comfort (1 Cor. 14:3).

We encourage believers who are not called into the office of a prophet to stay within the limit of edification, exhortation, and comfort. Believers who attempt to go beyond their level of grace without additional equipping will bring confusion to the body of Christ. Those who are recognized by the leadership of the assembly as *prophets* are the ones who have the authority to speak beyond the limit of edification, exhortation, and comfort.

The office of the prophet

The highest level in the prophetic realm is the office of the prophet.

> And God hath set some in the church, first apostles,
> secondarily prophets, thirdly teachers, after that miracles,
> then gifts of healings, helps, governments, diversities of
> tongues.
>
> —1 CORINTHIANS 12:28

The prophets will have the strongest utterances because they speak by the spirit of prophecy, the gift of prophecy, and also out of the strength of the prophet's office. They have the grace to speak messages that go beyond words of edification, exhortation, and comfort.

Prophets prophesy with more authority than other believers who have not been called to the office of the prophet. Their prophecies can carry revelation, direction, correction, confirmation, impartation, and activation. They minister to a wider scope of needs than believers who speak by the spirit of prophecy or the simple gift of prophecy.

The breadth and height of the prophetic reach extends far and wide and to the summit or pinnacle of heaven. The depth and length of the prophetic reach is full and comprehensive, complete and thorough. The Lord desires His church to walk in the breadth, length, depth, and height of the prophetic realm, and He installs men and women in the office of the prophet to make this possible. The prophet has the anointing by grace to minister and speak in higher, wider, and deeper ways.

There are levels of strength of the gift, depending upon the measure of grace received by the person who has the gift.

I believe that prophets should minister under authority and be recognized by the leadership of their local body of Christ because the Lord desires that all things be done decently and in order.

GOD'S GRACE, OUR BOUNDARY

I like the way a fellow minister states it. He says, "*Grace is God's ability, which is our boundary.*" In other words, you are limited by the amount of grace you have received from the Lord. Paul made this clear in his letter to the local church in Rome:

> For as we have many members in one body, but all the members do not have the same function, so we, being many, are one body in Christ, and individually members of one another. *Having then gifts differing according to the grace that is given to us, let us use them: if prophecy, let us prophesy in proportion to our faith*; or ministry, let us use it in our ministering; he who teaches, in teaching; he who exhorts, in exhortation; he who gives, with liberality; he who leads, with diligence; he who shows mercy, with cheerfulness.
> —ROMANS 12:4–8, NKJV, emphasis added

Every believer should operate in the prophetic realm in one or more of these prophetic levels. But our levels of grace differ. When the spirit of prophecy is strong in the local assembly, more believers will be able to operate in the different levels of prophecy.

You must discern your measure of grace and operate within its boundaries. All believers can prophesy, but all will not be able to operate in the highest level of the prophetic anointing—the office of the prophet. It is the highest and strongest level, and it will usher God's people into a greater degree of glory. It is this higher degree of the prophetic anointing that we will discuss at more length in this book.

Until the church begins to understand and walk in all the levels of prophecy—including this highest level, the office of the prophet—we will not see the greatest results and manifestations of the Holy Spirit in our midst. Jesus died, rose again, and sent the Holy Spirit so that we, God's people, might be perfected and matured into His image. Powerful prophetic utterances provide part of the direction for that maturing and perfecting process.

We should not settle for anything less than the fullest of what Jesus has provided for us. As we learn how to flow in the spirit of prophecy and the gift of prophecy, we will also learn how to walk in and receive from the ministry of the prophet. This is a grace gift to the body of Christ.

I cannot overemphasize the importance of prophecy. Churches should excel in it:

> Even so ye, forasmuch as ye are zealous of spiritual gifts, seek that ye may excel to the edifying of the church.
> —1 Corinthians 14:12

The prophetic level of your local church should not be mediocre, average, or subpar. People need to be activated and trained to flow in the spirit of prophecy. We must take time to teach in this area and make room for its operation. It will not happen by accident. We should have a strategy to raise the level of operation of the prophetic anointing within our local church.

Prophetic Administrations

To *administer* means to manage or supervise the execution, use, or conduct of. It also means to minister or serve. Scripture tells us that "there are differences of administrations, but the same Lord" (1 Cor. 12:5). In the context of prophecy, there are different ways to minister the prophetic anointing.

I have divided the prophetic anointing into three levels: (1) the spirit of prophecy, (2) the gift of prophecy, and (3) the office of the prophet. All represent administrations of the prophetic anointing with further specific administrations falling under the auspices of the office of prophet. Because the prophet has grace and authority to go beyond these first two levels, prophets can administer the prophetic anointing through rebuke, correction, direction, impartation, activation, confirmation, and revelation. Prophets can also minister helps, healing, miracles, and deliverance. We will be examining each of these in turn in this chapter and the next.

Did you know that there is an administration of healing that can come through prophets? I have seen people receive healing through prophetic utterances and the laying on of hands. I also have seen devils come out of people as they receive prophecy; this is an administration of deliverance through the prophetic anointing.

Elijah and Elisha both raised the dead and performed miracles of healing and provision. John the Baptist did no miracles, yet he was definitely a prophet of the Most High. (See John 10:41.) There is no record of Daniel performing miracles, yet he was strong in visions, dreams, and understanding.

The highest level in the prophetic realm is the office of the prophet.

All were prophets, but they flowed in different administrations. Moses was a prophet who was strong in administration and deliverance. Ezekiel and Zechariah were visionary prophets. Prophets are different depending on the measure of grace and giftings of the Holy Spirit. The prophet's office cannot be limited to one specific type or mode. Although there are certain characteristics and similarities we can look for to identify true prophets, there are also differences.

Some prophets are stronger in healing and miracles while others are stronger in visions and dreams. Some prophets are stronger in activation and impartation while others are stronger in confirmation. The prophetess is an administration of the prophetic anointing through a handmaiden of the Lord.

These different administrations or applications of prophecy reach different people. What one administration can't reach, another can.

Every administration has a time and purpose (Eccles. 3:1). It is important to acknowledge and receive all the different administrations of each office as they are expressed in the local church. Together, they comprise the Lord's body on the earth today.

Prophetic music

Another administration of the prophet's anointing is through music. There are prophets who function as psalmists and minstrels. David is a good example of a man who had this administration, and he is called the sweet psalmist of Israel (2 Sam. 23:1). David understood the importance of music in stirring up and maintaining the corporate flow of God's Spirit. The strength of the spirit of prophecy in our midst will always be determined by our level of worship. (See Revelation 19:10.)

I believe that everyone who leads worship or plays instruments in the house of the Lord should flow to some degree under a prophetic anointing. Look how David organized the worship leaders:

> Moreover David and the captains of the host separated to the service of the sons of Asaph, and of Heman, and of Jeduthun, who should prophesy with harps, with psalteries, and with cymbals.
> —1 CHRONICLES 25:1

All may not be prophets, but the spirit of prophecy can be strong enough in our churches whereby everyone can enter into the prophetic flow.

Psalmists and musicians who are prophets will sing and play instruments under strong prophetic anointing. This can bring impartation, activation, direction, confirmation, and revelation just as prophesying without music can. It is a different administration of the anointing. The Spirit of the Lord will use the vehicle of song and music to impart and establish gifts and anointings in the local assembly.

Revelation flows through this administration. Divine secrets are revealed as we flow in prophetic singing and music. "I will incline mine ear to a parable: I will open my dark saying upon the harp" (Ps. 49:4). Parables are the mysteries of God, and yet all of them do not remain mysteries, because it has been given unto us to know the mysteries of the kingdom (Matt. 13:11). I have found that congregations who flow in the worship/music administration of the prophetic anointing walk in a greater degree of revelation.

It is no wonder that the enemy fights music in the house of the Lord. Many pastors have a difficult time establishing the music department. I have seen churches struggle in this area more often than not. The enemy tries to bring confusion in this area of ministry. The enemy desires to block the flow of revelation that would come through prophetic music.

Until the church begins to understand and walk in all the levels of prophecy, we will not see the greatest results and manifestations of the Holy Spirit in our midst.

Prophets make great praise leaders. Some prophets have the misconception that praise and worship is beneath them. They say, "Give me the pulpit because I am a prophet." But I say that the prophets should return to praise and worship. Not all prophets can flow in this administration. Some can't carry a tune in a bucket. But there are prophets who are definitely called to this area. We need to receive this administration into our local assemblies.

The company of prophets under Samuel prophesied with instruments and music (1 Sam. 10:5). So do not be surprised to see many prophets being trained in church music departments, where they will develop a listening ear and the sensitivity they need to hear the voice of the Lord accurately through music.

Prophetic helps

Prophets are helpers of a specific kind. Haggai and Zechariah were prophets sent by God to *help* Zerubbabel and Jeshua rebuild the temple and reestablish the priesthood:

> Then the prophets, Haggai the prophet, and Zechariah the son of Iddo, prophesied unto the Jews that were in Judah and Jerusalem in the name of the God of Israel, even unto them.
>
> Then rose up Zerubbabel the son of Shealtiel, and Jeshua the son of Jozadak, and began to build the house of God which is at Jerusalem: *and with them were the prophets of God helping them.*
>
> —EZRA 5:1–2, emphasis added

In general, prophets help build the house of the Lord. The people had felt it was not time to build the house of the Lord (Hag. 1:2). They felt this way because of the difficult conditions under which they were trying to build it. They had just returned from seventy years of captivity in Babylon. They were busy building their own houses and returning to the land (v. 4). There was also considerable opposition to the work from their adversaries. The people of the land were trying to weaken the hands of the people of Judah, troubling them in the building process (Ezra 4:4). As a result, the work of building the temple was badly hindered. The prophets came to help with the work and to reverse the opposition.

We should note here one of the major differences between Old Testament prophetic ministry and New Testament prophetic ministry. Old

Testament saints depended more upon the prophets because they did not have the infilling of the Spirit as we do. New Testament ministry confirms what the Spirit of God is leading us to do. Remember, we are led by the Spirit of God, not by prophets.

However, even though we are filled with the Spirit, we still need confirmation and prophetic ministry. Spirit-filled believers still need edification, exhortation, and comfort. We still need the witnesses the Lord has provided to be established in the will of God, which will cause us to be confirmed unto the end.

SATANIC OPPOSITION

Satanic opposition will come when men rise up to build the house of God. Many local assemblies are stifled and hindered because of evil spirits opposing the work. The prophetic anointing gives discernment as to the source of problems that we may encounter. Prophets have the ability to discern and identify the spirits that are hindering a person or a ministry.

In the time of the temple rebuilding, the people of the Lord, unaware of the satanic nature of the opposition, left off building the house of the Lord. The leaders, Zerubbabel and Jeshua, became discouraged. The house of the Lord lay waste (Hag. 1:4).

The people and the leaders needed prophetic help, so the Lord sent Haggai and Zechariah to help them finish the work. First, there was rebuke for not continuing the work in spite of the opposition. Rebuke is unpleasant but sometimes necessary in building the house of the Lord. Prophets have the anointing and authority to rebuke when necessary. Rebuke can be part of the exhortation function of prophecy.

Old Testament saints depended more upon the prophets because they did not have the infilling of the Spirit as we do.

I have seen local assemblies being hindered by satanic opposition. The result was the people stopped using their faith and became apathetic concerning the work of the Lord. I have witnessed prophets minister in rebuke with the result being a complete transformation in the people. Repentance and obedience resulted, and the work of the Lord prospered.

Destroying satanic mountains

The opposition to the rebuilding of the temple and reestablishing of the priesthood was satanic. In a vision, the prophet Zechariah saw Satan standing to oppose this work:

> And he shewed me Joshua the high priest standing before the angel of the LORD, and Satan standing at his right hand to resist him.
> And the LORD said unto Satan, The LORD rebuke thee, O Satan; even the LORD that hath chosen Jerusalem rebuke thee: is not this a brand plucked out of the fire?
> —ZECHARIAH 3:1–2

Haggai and Zechariah did not just rebuke the people and Satan, but they also exhorted the people and the leadership to complete the work. Zechariah gave the word of the Lord to Zerubbabel, the governor and overseer in charge of the work:

> Then he answered and spake unto me, saying, This is the word of the LORD unto Zerubbabel, saying, Not by might, nor by power, but by my spirit, saith the LORD of hosts.

> Who art thou, O great mountain? before Zerubbabel
> thou shalt become a plain: and he shall bring forth the
> headstone thereof with shoutings, crying, Grace, grace
> unto it.
>
> —ZECHARIAH 4:6–7

The satanic opposition to this work was a mountain to Zerubbabel. He could not get past it in his own strength. The prophet encouraged him to depend upon the Spirit of the Lord to overcome this mountain. The mountain would fall before Zerubbabel because of the grace of God upon him, and then the work would be completed.

True prophetic ministry is not sent to control and dominate leadership but to help it.

Satanic opposition to the work of the Lord can appear to be a mountain. Many leaders need prophetic ministry to destroy and get past the mountain of opposition they face. The Lord has commanded many leaders to build, and opposition as large as a mountain has blocked their way. Obstacles do not mean a leader is not obeying the Lord. Many leaders become discouraged and need prophetic help. Prophets can minister strength and encouragement to God's leaders, enabling them to complete the work of the Lord.

Sometimes the mountain is financial. Sometimes opposition can come from people within the congregation. The word of the Lord from the prophets will help destroy these mountains. It is no wonder Satan hates prophets and tries to alienate them from leadership, especially from pastors. Satan knows that the anointing upon the prophet will destroy the mountains he places in the way to hinder the work of the Lord. I have witnessed congregations and leaders turned around and brought into victory through prophetic ministry. Mountains are destroyed and the work prospers.

REBUILDING AFTER OPPOSITION

Haggai prophesied strength into the leadership and into people:

> Yet now be strong, O Zerubbabel, saith the LORD; and be strong, O Joshua, son of Josedech, the high priest; and be strong, all ye people of the land, saith the LORD, and work: for I am with you, saith the LORD of hosts.
>
> —HAGGAI 2:4

The word they received from the prophet gave them the strength they needed to build the Lord's house. It takes strength to defeat the powers of darkness and build the house of the Lord. The prophet brings strength and confirmation. Without this strength, the people will become weary and often faint. The weak hands need to be strengthened, and the feeble knees confirmed (Isa. 35:3).

> And the elders of the Jews builded, and they prospered through the prophesying of Haggai the prophet and Zechariah the son of Iddo. And they builded, and finished it, according to the commandment of the God of Israel.
>
> —EZRA 6:14

The elders represent leadership. As the leaders hearkened unto the voice of the prophets, they prospered and finished the work. The prophets were not sent to be in charge of the work as coleaders. The leaders were the ones in charge of the work. The prophets were sent to *help* the leadership. If the leaders listened to the prophets, they would succeed; if they refused, they would fail. True prophetic ministry is not sent to control and dominate leadership but to help it. Prophets can be in leadership positions in local assemblies, and there are many pastors who are also prophets. However, if a prophet is not a pastor, he will be sent to help a pastor. Prophets are sent to help discern direction, to build and to bless the work of the Lord, not to control and dictate decisions.

> Believe in the LORD your God, so shall ye be established; believe his prophets, so shall ye prosper.
> —2 CHRONICLES 20:20

Quite simply, the work of the Lord prospers through prophecy. Your life will prosper through prophecy as well. Since a lack of prosperity and blessing is often the result of evil spirits, we need prophets to break and destroy demonic kingdoms through prophecy.

Just as Ezekiel prophesied to the dry bones, and skin and sinews came upon them, giving form and strength to an exceeding great army (Ezek. 37:8–10), so too strength is imparted into people when prophets prophesy. The result will be stronger churches, stronger leaders, stronger anointings, stronger praise, stronger giving, and stronger evangelism. People can be prophesied out of weakness into strength. If pastors want to have strong churches, they must allow prophets to minister and to prophesy freely. Local churches will then become strong enough to break through all opposition and to prosper.

chapter three

DISCERNING YOUR PART
IN THE PLAN OF GOD

With revelation, apostles and prophets minister the purposes of the Lord for the church. The anointing gives them special insight into divine purposes. They have the ability to make the saints see their part and place in the purposes of God.

> ...which in other ages was not made known unto the sons of men, as it is now revealed unto his holy apostles and prophets by the Spirit.... And to make all men see what is the fellowship of the mystery.
>
> —Ephesians 3:5, 9

We all need to know our fellowship (part) in the plan of God. As individuals, churches, and families, we need to know what our role is in the plan of God. Prophets deal with eternal purposes. (See Ephesians 3:11.) The eternal plans and purposes ordained by the Lord from before the foundation of the world apply to every person. Each and every one of us has been born with a part in the eternal purposes of God. We can choose to walk in that purpose or reject it through disobedience and rebellion—or through ignorance.

Prophets minister revelation concerning our fellowship (part) of the mystery (purpose) of the Lord, and those who have a desire to know and fulfill the will of the Lord need to avail themselves of true prophetic ministry. The enemy attempts to keep us ignorant of our part in the purposes of God. He tries to divert us from the will of God. He wants to destroy us and interfere with the establishment of the kingdom of God in the earth.

Therefore, to reject the ministry of prophets is to reject the revelation the Lord desires to give us regarding our eternal purpose. As we honor and draw from the anointing of the prophet, we will walk in greater revelation of the purposes of the Lord. In other words, the prophet has been given as a gift to the body of Christ to bless us and perfect us. We can never be perfected without a revelation of the purposes of God.

FULFILL YOUR MINISTRY

Another way of saying that each of us was born with a part to play in God's eternal purpose is to say that we each have a destiny or a ministry to fulfill. Paul was referring to this when he wrote to a member of the Colossian church:

> And say to Archippus, Take heed to the ministry which thou hast received in the Lord, that thou fulfil it.
> —COLOSSIANS 4:17

Prophets help us fulfill our ministries by imparting the revelation we need to know concerning the will of the Lord. Ignorance of the will of the Lord will hinder people from fulfilling their ministries. Many people spend too much of their time operating in the wrong places and doing the wrong things simply because they do not know the will of the Lord.

We are not called to do anything and everything, but rather, we are called to fulfill a specific function within the body of Christ. The saints need to be fitly joined together and every part functioning properly (Eph. 4:16). I believe that prophets are the primary ones who can help us find our places in the body and learn to function properly, thus fulfilling the will of the Lord for the church.

Prophets in the local church

The saints learn from prophetic revelation, and they are "comforted":

> Let the prophets speak two or three, and let the other judge. If any thing be revealed to another that sitteth by, let the first hold his peace. For ye may all prophesy one by one, that all may learn, and all may be comforted.
> —1 CORINTHIANS 14:29–31

These verses are in reference to prophets ministering by revelation in the local church. Notice that prophets receive revelation, and they can all prophesy (speak forth the revelation) "that all may learn, and all may be comforted." Thus, prophetic revelation does not bring fear but comfort. The Phillips translation says that "everyone will have his faith stimulated" (v. 31). Another word for *comfort* is *encouragement*.

The enemy attempts to keep us ignorant of our part in the purposes of God.

Often when one prophet is ministering, another prophet will begin to receive revelation as well. As the anointing flows, it will stir up others in their prophetic gift. If you are a prophet, you know what I mean. Prophets will find their gift stirred as they associate with other prophets. It should not be unusual for two or three prophets to speak out in sequence in a meeting of a local fellowship. And as one of them ministers, the others are to judge what is being said. Therefore, prophetic revelation is subject to being weighed by others.

Local assemblies that allow prophets to minister freely will achieve a greater degree of revelation, spiritual knowledge, comfort, and encouragement as they move toward fulfilling God's purposes.

PROPHETIC REVELATION

Before God does anything, He first reveals it to His servants the prophets. You have heard this line quoted often:

> Surely the Lord GOD will do nothing, but he *revealeth* his secret unto his servants the prophets.
>
> —AMOS 3:7, emphasis added

Prophetic revelation can come in the form of dreams, visions, or the direct words of the Lord. Prophets are also known as "seers" because they see beforehand what the Lord will do, and they then speak forth what they have seen in dreams or visions or have heard in the spirit.

Many people spend too much of their time operating in the wrong places and doing the wrong things simply because they do not know the will of the Lord.

When a prophet speaks out what he or she has seen in the spirit, the Lord hastens to perform the words of the prophet because it is really His word and His will expressed through one of His servants. Because prophetic revelation gives us insight into the plans and purposes of God, it makes us able to bring our lives into agreement with what the Lord is doing.

> See then that ye walk circumspectly, not as fools, but as wise, redeeming the time, because the days are evil. Wherefore be ye not unwise, but understanding what the will of the Lord is.
>
> —EPHESIANS 5:15–17

It is not the will of the Lord for us to be ignorant of His plans and purposes. When we know the will of the Lord, we are then able to redeem the time and accomplish His intended will. Time will not be wasted on things the Lord has not called us to do.

Prophetic ministry is the means by which God will bring us the revelation of the will of the Lord for our lives and churches. When prophetic ministry is lacking, darkness and confusion concerning the will of the Lord will result. In other words, the will of the Lord is not only seen and heard in the spirit by prophets, but it is also spoken and activated by prophets.

When the Spirit of God moves and the prophets prophesy, light comes. The illumination power of revelation penetrates the darkness of confusion. The church begins to discern the will of the Lord. As soon as the word of the Lord is spoken, confusion and ignorance depart. How exciting it is to see saints receive prophetic ministry and their lives and ministries come into form. Without prophetic ministry, darkness and confusion are often present. With prophetic ministry, believers receive clarity of vision and energy of purpose.

We can know the general will of God through reading the Word of God. We need to study the Bible for this reason. However, the specific will of the Lord for individuals, families, churches, and nations can only be received through revelation, and this entails prophetic ministry.

I have received personal prophecy over a consistent period of time that has helped me to know the will of God for my life and ministry. This has enabled me to channel my time and energy into the perfect will of God for my life. It has eliminated double-mindedness and instability and given me the faith and assurance I need to fulfill the purposes of God for my life.

Local assemblies that allow prophets to minister freely will achieve a greater degree of revelation, spiritual knowledge, comfort, and encouragement.

I am not recommending that we replace an individual's personal responsibility to pray and seek the will of the Lord with the words of prophets. Each one of us is still responsible to pray and hear from the Lord concerning His will for our lives. But the prophets can minister revelation to us, giving us a clearer picture and understanding of what the Lord is leading us to do.

PROPHETIC IMPARTATION

One of the abilities of prophets is to impart blessings to other people. We see this in Romans 1:11, where the apostle Paul said, "For I long to see you, that I may impart unto you some spiritual gift, to the end ye may be established." Paul had a desire to come to the church at Rome so that he could impart spiritual gifts to the church members and help them be established in mature strength. It was the anointing of the prophet that gave him the ability to impart spiritual gifts and anointings into people through prophetic utterances and through the laying on of hands.

Timothy received an impartation of a gift and the anointing of God through prophecy and the laying on of hands:

> Neglect not the gift that is in thee, which was given thee by prophecy, with the laying on of the hands of the presbytery.
>
> —1 TIMOTHY 4:14

There was a transference of spiritual power, authority, ability, and grace. Paul then told Timothy not to neglect what he had received through impartation.

All of us need impartations of the anointing. You can receive some things directly from God; other things will come through the channel of another individual. Although most people received gifts and callings when they were born again and baptized in the Holy Spirit, additional anointings can come through the avenue of laying on of hands and prophecy.

When this avenue is lacking, the result will be a lack of strong ministries and anointings in the local assembly. We need this blessing of impartation, given to us by the Lord Jesus Christ. It is important that the body of Christ discern and embrace this function of prophets. Otherwise, we will miss the deposit of anointings and gifts that could have come through prophetic impartation. All of the ministry gifts, especially those who are young, can benefit from receiving additional supernatural gifts and anointings through prophesying and praying with the laying on of hands.

I personally feel that every ministry gift needs the ministry of the prophet. As we allow prophets to minister unto us by the Spirit of

God, the Lord can impart or deposit things into our lives. We need these impartations to make our ministries effective. Some ministry gifts lack because they have not come into contact with or allowed prophets to prophesy into their lives. In other words, what may be lacking in the operation of a ministry gift in the local assembly may be a lack of prophetic ministry. Without prophetic impartation, individuals will not have the necessary equipping they need for fruitful and powerful ministries.

This ability to impart is different from the simple gift of prophecy, which is meant for edification, exhortation, and comfort. Those who have the simple gift of prophecy may not have the ability to impart the way the prophet does. A person with the office of prophet does more than prophesy; he or she also imparts. You can see the difference when a prophet prophesies. The words will do more than edify, exhort, and comfort. They will also impart spiritual grace into individuals and assemblies.

Every ministry gift needs the ministry of the prophet.

Equipping the saints for ministry is more than just teaching them how to do it; it also involves impartation. The Word of God is effective, but it is not enough by itself. In fact, it says so through all the examples of prophetic activity that it includes for our instruction. In other words, when you equip someone, you not only give them the Word of God, but you also impart into them the necessary gifts they need to do the work of the ministry, and the prophet has a vital part in equipping the saints for the work of the ministry.

A good example of impartation is when Elijah was taken up into heaven and his mantle fell so that Elisha could retrieve it (2 Kings 2). As a direct result, Elisha received a double portion of Elijah's spirit.

Another example of an impartation was when Moses, through the laying on of hands, imparted wisdom into Joshua (Deut. 34:9).

You can see that prophets do more than just prophesy. They also impart, transfer, and transmit anointings and gifts as the Spirit of God leads.

Establishment

According to Romans 1:11, the result of this impartation is establishment. You can be established, firm and strong, in your ministry as the prophets impart unto you through prophecy and the laying on of hands.

It is quite likely that the reason many gifts are not established in local churches is because of the lack of the prophetic anointing, which releases impartation, which in turn causes God's provision to be established in local assemblies.

I believe that every local assembly needs the prophet's ministry of impartation. Without the anointing of the prophet, certain things will not be established, strong, or made firm in the local church.

Power

Another direct result of prophetic impartation is spiritual power. The Lord Jesus gave His disciples power over unclean spirits and sickness (Matt. 10:1). He imparted this power to them.

In 1 Samuel 10, we find impartation coming to Saul as he met the company of prophets prophesying. The Spirit of the Lord came into him, and this resulted in his being "turned into another man" (v. 6). When individuals come into contact with those who have a prophetic anointing, there will be a powerful impartation.

Character

A word needs to be added about the importance of good, upstanding, personal character. The Word of God tells us to lay hands suddenly upon no man (1 Tim. 5:22). Prophets should lay hands on and prophesy impartation to people who have been faithful and have developed good character. Individuals who have not developed Christlike character should not receive impartation of this kind, because they will end up operating in the gifts and callings of God with bad character. When people go forth in ministry with character flaws, eventual falling and possible reproach on the ministry can result.

PROPHETIC ACTIVATION

The prophet's anointing carries with it the ability to activate. Prophets have the ability through prophesying not only to impart but also to stir up and ignite ministries and gifts within individuals. The breath of God is released through prophesying, and life is imparted and activated.

The prophet Ezekiel was commanded by the Lord to prophesy to dry bones:

> So I prophesied as he commanded me, and the breath came into them, and they lived, and stood up upon their feet, an exceeding great army.
> —EZEKIEL 37:10

These dry bones represented the house of Israel. As Ezekiel prophesied, the bones came together. The prophet has the ability to prophesy people into their right position within the body of Christ.

As Ezekiel prophesied, sinews and flesh came upon the bones. Sinews represent strength, and skin represents form. The necessary components are prophesied into proper form, and then life and strength are added, all through the prophetic ministry.

With prophetic activation, local assemblies will have greater strength and proper form. People will come into their right positions. When people are out of position in the local assembly, the result is confusion.

The prophetic ministry can also activate miracles, healings, and signs and wonders within the local assembly. All of the gifts of the Spirit are activated through prophetic ministry.

If there is a lack of anointing within a local assembly, the prophet can activate and bring back to life whatever is dormant and dead. Many individuals have gifts in them that need to be stirred up (activated). If they have not been able to stir up the gifts themselves, their gifts can be activated through prophetic ministry.

Many saints have callings from the womb (Jer. 1:5). There is a particular time when that call is supposed to be activated. The prophet has the ability through the Spirit of God to activate that particular call according to the will of the Spirit of God.

Equipping the saints for ministry is more than just teaching them how to do it; it also involves impartation.

The prophet also has the ability to position people. Many churches are disorganized and the members are not correctly joined together in the spirit. The prophet has the ability to speak order into the house of the Lord.

In short, the prophet has the ability to speak life into a situation. This is activation. This will raise up the army of God. Through prophetic utterances, people are positioned into proper rank. This may come through rebuke, or correction, or by simply prophesying people into their rightful position.

Scripture states that the gifts and callings of God are without repentance (Rom. 11:29). Some people may feel they have lost their gift or that God has taken it back when it simply needs activation because it is dormant. The gift may be dormant because of neglect or blockages.

I often find myself around prophets who can speak into my life and stir up and reactivate the gifts that I have. Prophets have the ability to activate and stir up your gifts too. This will "put sinews and muscles upon you" and make the gift strong.

Activating ministries

> Now there were in the church that was at Antioch certain prophets and teachers; as Barnabas, and Simeon that was called Niger, and Lucius of Cyrene, and Manaen, which had been brought up with Herod the tetrarch, and Saul.
>
> As they ministered to the Lord, and fasted, the Holy Ghost said, Separate me Barnabas and Saul [Paul] for the work whereunto I have called them.
>
> And when they had fasted and prayed, and laid their hands on them, they sent them away.
>
> —Acts 13:1–3

Prophetic ministry activates ministries and sends them forth. For Barnabas and Paul, the call to the apostleship was already present, but it needed to be activated. At a certain time or season it was time for the call to be activated and for the men to be sent forth as apostles. These verses seem to imply that prophetic ministry, through the laying on of hands, was instrumental in the releasing of Paul and Barnabas to begin their ministry to the Gentiles. Although verse 4 states they were sent forth by the Holy Ghost, and the Holy Ghost is the One who calls, anoints, and sends forth ministries, the Holy Ghost uses human channels to accomplish this work. It was important to have prophetic ministry in order to activate and release the ministry gifts of Barnabas and Paul.

Both prophetic impartation and activation are needed when ministry gifts are launched into ministry. Those who do not avail themselves of prophetic ministry will often be released prematurely, without the necessary activation and impartation of anointings and spiritual gifts. The call may be there, but the ability to fulfill it may not.

Prophetic ministry is the means by which God will bring us the revelation of the will of the Lord for our lives and churches.

As we know, Paul and Barnabas were released into a strong apostolic ministry because of the administration of prophets in the church at Antioch. In this hour, the Lord is raising up more Antioch churches to release strong ministries into the earth.

PROPHETIC CONFIRMATION

According to Webster, to *confirm* means to make firm, to strengthen, to give new assurance to, to remove doubt. When something is firm, it is securely or solidly fixed in place. It will be set, definite, and not easily moved or disturbed. When something is confirmed, it will be marked by long continuance and likely to persist. This is the will of God for the saints. The ministry of the prophet has been set in the church by and for the confirmation of the saints.

> And Judas and Silas, being prophets also themselves, exhorted the brethren with many words, and confirmed them.
>
> —ACTS 15:32

When prophets minister, confirmation will be the result. The saints will be "steadfast, immovable, always abounding in the work of the Lord" (1 Cor. 15:58, NKJV). It was necessary for Judas and Silas to minister confirmation to this particular church because of false teaching. The souls of the saints were being subverted (Acts 15:24), which means they were being overturned or overthrown from their foundation, weakened or ruined by degrees. They had become destabilized. When saints are unstable, they will not abound in the work of the Lord. After they received prophetic ministry, these churches were established in the faith. They were made firm and strengthened concerning their salvation.

Two or three witnesses

It is a spiritual principle that the truth is established by the confirmation of two or three witnesses.

> This is the third time I am coming to you. In the mouth of two or three witnesses shall every word be established.
>
> —2 CORINTHIANS 13:1

Prophets can provide another witness. You may have a witness in your spirit concerning a certain matter and yet not be established in the fact that it is from the Lord. The Lord in His mercy has provided prophetic ministry as another witness so that we may be established in the will of God for our lives.

The Word of God tells us to prove all things (1 Thess. 5:21). Anything that is from the Lord can be proven. When the will of

God is confirmed by prophetic ministry, there will be assurance and steadfastness instead of wavering and doubting. The testimony of Jesus is the spirit of prophecy (Rev. 19:10). Prophecy is a witness (testimony). This is the very spirit of all prophecy: to give the confirmation and witness of Jesus.

Dissolving of doubts

We find in Scripture this interesting description of Daniel, who was one of the premier prophets:

> Forasmuch as an excellent spirit, and knowledge, and understanding, interpreting of dreams, and shewing of hard sentences, and dissolving of doubts, were found in the same Daniel...
>
> —Daniel 5:12

Because we more often concentrate our attention on his other qualities, we seldom notice that *Daniel had the ability to dissolve doubts*. Evidently, the prophet's anointing will dissolve doubts, causing persons who receive prophetic ministry to walk in a greater degree of faith and assurance. They will have a clearer understanding of the will of God. They will receive confirmation, as I mentioned above, but they will also have doubts removed from their minds.

Daniel was able to remove all doubt and confusion from the king by interpreting his dreams. Saints who struggle with doubts and hesitancy will benefit from anointed prophetic confirmation. Their doubts will disappear, their faith level will be elevated, and they will be able to move forward effectively, without hesitation. Prophetic confirmation will destroy double-mindedness and will result in stability instead of instability, making it possible for them to be confirmed unto the end.

Who shall also confirm you unto the end, that ye may be
blameless in the day of our Lord Jesus Christ.

—1 CORINTHIANS 1:8

SPIRIT-FILLED ORDINATION SERVICES

Ordination is the act of officially investing someone with ministerial
or priestly authority. In Acts 6:6, the apostles laid hands upon the
first deacons to set them in their offices. This was also an impartation of apostolic anointing that released Stephen and Philip into
miracle ministries. In the early church, bishops and elders were also
ordained in this fashion and set in their respective offices.

*Saints who struggle with doubts and hesitancy will benefit from
anointed prophetic confirmation.*

After the death of the early apostles, the church lost most of its
power, and ordination became largely ceremonial. But today, the
Lord is restoring the reality and power of ordination to set various
ministries in the church. Through apostolic and prophetic ministry,
anointings can be imparted into those who are being ordained. (See
1 Timothy 4:14.) In the ordination services of our church, we call for
the prophets to come and prophesy over those who are candidates for
ordination. We call this prophetic presbytery. I believe that prophetic
presbytery is necessary in this hour to release strong ministry gifts
and that as a result, ordination services should no longer be merely
ceremonial but full of the power and anointing of the Holy Spirit.
Allowing the prophets to flow in this administration will launch
stronger ministries.

By allowing and encouraging different prophetic administrations, we will see more of the benefits of the Spirit established in the house of the Lord. We cannot become addicted to one type of administration but must receive all that the Lord has for us. In this way, we can be filled with all the fullness of God. (See Ephesians 3:19.)

We see that prophets can minister and provide help through revelation, impartation, activation, and confirmation. Through these different administrations, prophets can speak and minister to the saints with the authority that is given by grace. God has provided these spiritual helps for the church that we might be changed into the image of Jesus Christ. Thank God for the different functions of prophets. May we release and receive this important ministry and through it draw from the grace of God that has been deposited among us.

chapter four

UNDERSTANDING THE OFFICE OF THE PROPHET

THE CHURCH IS a prophetic community. God has set prophets in the church because they are important to the health and strength of the local assembly.

Carrying tremendous authority and having the capacity to bring great blessing to those who receive their ministry, prophets should function under the new covenant law, under which they are accepted as bearers of one of the ministry gifts established by God to perfect believers. (See Ephesians 4:11–12.) No longer should prophets have to function under the old covenant mind-set of rejection, persecution, and exile. Prophets need to be integrated into the fabric of the life of a healthy church.

PROPHETIC AUTHORITY

Jeremiah gives a picture of the authority of a prophet:

> See, I have this day set thee over the nations and over the
> kingdoms, to root out, and to pull down, and to destroy,
> and to throw down, to build, and to plant.
>
> —JEREMIAH 1:10

This is true not only for Old Testament prophets but also for
present-day prophets. When prophets speak, the utterances that
come from their mouths are charged with the anointing and power of
God. They carry divine authority. This authority is given to prophets
by the grace of God, and it is given for two reasons:

1. For the destruction of Satan's kingdom

2. For the establishment of the kingdom of God

In this chapter, we will be exploring the specific ways in which
prophets function to tear down the kingdom of darkness and bring
in the kingdom of God's light. The kingdom of darkness produces
sin, rebellion, sickness, and poverty, but the kingdom of God is righteousness, peace, and joy in the Holy Ghost (Rom. 14:17).

All ministry gifts are called to and responsible for establishing
righteousness, peace, and joy in the Holy Ghost, but the authority
of the prophets enables them to root out, pull down, destroy, and
throw down the works of the devil. Prophets also have the authority
to build and plant the kingdom of God. Although the end result of
coming against Satan's kingdom is to make room for the kingdom
of God, it often seems like twice as much emphasis is given to
destroying the kingdom of darkness as opposed to building up the
kingdom of God.

Those who operate in the prophetic anointing seem to find themselves being thrown into warfare frequently and being in direct
conflict with the powers of darkness. The prophetic anointing is

often *confrontational*. An example of this confrontational anointing is Elijah, who challenged and confronted the powers of idolatry on Mount Carmel. Because of the prophet's office, he was able to pull down the stronghold of Baal that ruled Israel. As a result of Elijah's ministry, eventual judgment came upon the house of Ahab.

Through the utterances of prophets, evil spirits are rooted out of their dwelling places. Those who have the office of the prophet speak with more authority than believers who prophesy by the spirit of prophecy or by the simple gift of prophecy. The words of the prophets are like an ax laid at the root of the trees (Luke 3:9). By their divinely inspired words, every tree that does not bear fruit is cut down and cast into the fire. In the midst of true prophetic ministry, only what is fruitful and productive to the kingdom will stand.

Pulling down strongholds

> For the weapons of our warfare are not carnal, but mighty through God to the pulling down of strong holds.
> —2 CORINTHIANS 10:4

Jeremiah the prophet was given authority over kingdoms and nations. Prophets have authority over demonic kingdoms. Satan sets up demonic strongholds in individuals, families, churches, cities, and nations. The prophet's anointing is a spiritual weapon in the hand of the Lord to pull down strongholds.

The kingdom of darkness produces sin, rebellion, sickness, and poverty, but the kingdom of God is righteousness, peace, and joy in the Holy Ghost.

I have seen deliverance come through prophesying to individuals, families, and local assemblies. I have seen people weeping and broken after receiving prophetic utterances. Prophets usually carry a strong deliverance anointing. As a result, the ministry of the prophet provides deliverance and the pulling down of strongholds.

> And by a prophet the LORD brought Israel out of Egypt,
> and by a prophet was he preserved.
> —HOSEA 12:13

The prophet has the responsibility to minister the word of God just as much as he or she prophesies by the Spirit of God. This combined anointing provides the ability to bring deliverance to God's people in a unique way. I have witnessed pastors struggle with strongholds in local assemblies that they were unable to pull down. The pastor's anointing is important, but it may take a different anointing to pull down certain strongholds. This does not elevate the prophet above the pastor in the local assembly, for we are all laborers together with God. However, pastors need to discern the importance of the prophet's anointing to the pulling down of strongholds.

Rooting out evil

> But he answered and said, Every plant, which my heavenly
> Father hath not planted, shall be rooted up.
> —MATTHEW 15:13

Jesus was referring to the religious leaders of that day. His ministry was causing them to be offended, and because they were offended, an uprooting was taking place in the spirit. When people are uprooted through prophetic ministry, they will often be offended. Eventually, the entire system of religion in Judah and Jerusalem was uprooted and the Jewish people were scattered.

The enemy had planted tares among the wheat. (See Matthew 13.) The enemy can plant certain people in local assemblies to cause confusion and to harm the work of the Lord. Prophets are the ones who have the anointing to root them out.

If the troublemakers are rooted out without the anointing, damage can result. This is why the Lord told His servants not to attempt to gather the tares, lest while gathering the tares, they "root up also the wheat with them" (Matt. 13:29).

The prophetic anointing is often confrontational.

Rooting out a spirit or demonic influence is not something that can be done in the flesh. A spirit or demonic influence must be rooted out in the power of the Spirit of God.

> His confidence shall be rooted out of his tabernacle, and it shall bring him to the king of terrors.
>
> —JOB 18:14

There are times when the prophet is unaware, in the natural, of what is being accomplished in the spirit. The actual rooting out may not occur until after the prophet has departed the scene, sometimes even years later. What is taking place in the natural may be the result of what has happened in the spirit years ago. What we see in the natural is only a reflection of what is taking place, or what has already taken place, in the spirit.

Destroying the works of the devil

True prophets are able to destroy the works of the devil. Many people, including pastors, fear prophetic ministry because it is so powerful. However, the righteous pastor should not be afraid, for true prophetic ministry will only destroy what is of the devil; it will never destroy what is of the Lord. True prophetic ministry will establish the things of the Spirit while destroying the things of the devil.

Unfortunately, much of what goes on in local assemblies is fleshly and even sometimes demonic. The prophet's ministry will destroy what is fleshly and demonic and establish holiness and purity in the house of the Lord. Prophets have a hatred for what God hates (Ps. 139:21–22). This is why prophets will often be criticized for not being more "tolerant."

The prophetic gift leaves no room for compromise. In fact, a compromising prophet will soon lose his or her effectiveness and eventually will be judged by the Lord. This is not to say that prophets have the right to be offensive or to minister in the flesh. Prophets must minister in the Spirit at all times. A prophet who tries to minister in the flesh will end up destroying and damaging that which is of the Lord instead of that which is of the devil. It is the same with any ministry gift. To minister in any way in the flesh causes reproach and damage.

The ministry of the prophet provides deliverance and the pulling down of strongholds.

True prophets will always have love and compassion for people but a corresponding hatred and intolerance for the works of the devil. Do not mistake hatred and intolerance for the works of the devil for being hard or judgmental, which is a fleshly response. We must discern between the operation of the flesh and the administration of the Holy Spirit. Without proper discernment and understanding, we will misjudge prophets and reject them, thus depriving the body of Christ of a very important ministry gift.

Throwing down idolatry

> And it shall come to pass, that like as I have watched over them, to pluck up, and to break down, and to throw down, and to destroy, and to afflict; so will I watch over them, to build, and to plant, saith the LORD.
>
> —JEREMIAH 31:28

The nation of Israel was commanded to enter Canaan and throw down the altars of the heathen. They were supposed to root out the nation of Canaan for their iniquity. Israel had to dispossess the Canaanites before they could enter and possess the Promised Land. Notice that before building and planting come rooting out and throwing down. This is an unpleasant part of ministry, but it is necessary nonetheless.

The prophet's anointing is like this; it is one of confrontation and warfare. First come confrontation and warfare; then come building and planting. Many a prophet has pulled back from confronting evil because of soulish fear and intimidation. Warfare is unpleasant to the soul. However, if a prophet allows the anointing to change him or her "into another man" (1 Sam. 10:6), the strength of the anointing will prevail over the drawing back of one's soul and cause one to be able to rise up and throw down the altars of sin (Hosea 8:11).

Often in ministry, prophets will not understand why that which they are ministering is going in a certain direction. In the spirit, prophets may encounter rebellion, control, witchcraft, and pride in an assembly without knowing in the natural anything about what is going on in the congregation. Sometimes the direction is the total opposite of where they started ministering in the Word. The anointing and leading of the Holy Spirit will cause prophets to hit areas of sin and rebellion in the spirit without knowledge in the natural.

AUTHORITY TO BUILD

Besides destroying, uprooting, pulling down, and throwing down the works of the devil, the prophet also builds up the body of Christ. This is their ministry of edification, exhortation, and comfort. Prophets have a strong hatred for the works of the devil, but they also have a genuine love and compassion for God's people, and the saints will be built up and edified through true prophetic ministry. When the church is built up in this way, the gates of hell will not be able to prevail against it.

We always need to remember that the purpose of tearing down strongholds is to build up the kingdom of God. Spiritual warfare is not an end but rather a means to an end. Those who have been called to prophetic ministry must always keep their focus on the goal, which is to build up the church.

It is possible to lose focus. There is no guarantee of pure motives. If the prophets lose focus, they end up doing considerable damage to the work of the Lord. Sometimes prophets develop what I refer to as a "blasting" mentality. They just want to blast everything that is not like God.

Remember, John the Baptist's mission was to prepare a people for the coming of the Lord. He spoke against wickedness and sin, but he also announced the arrival of the kingdom of God. In the same way, prophets must concern themselves not only with the works of the enemy but also with the needs of the people. They must balance their ministry with love and compassion, and they must avoid ministering in a harsh, critical, or bitter spirit. They have a responsibility to minister the Word in love. They have a responsibility to build up the Lord's house.

Planted to flourish

> Those that be planted in the house of the LORD shall flourish in the courts of our God.
>
> —PSALM 92:13

When people are exposed to true prophetic ministry, they will be *planted* in the house of the Lord. Those who are planted will flourish in every way. To be *planted* means to be rooted and grounded. People in prophetic ministry can uproot what the enemy has planted, and they can plant in local assemblies what has been ordained by the Lord.

In local churches, I have witnessed people coming with a hesitancy to be planted. They may waver, and they may not be dependable to help in the work of the Lord. Through the prophet's anointing, a prophet can minister strength and certainty to such hesitant saints and establish them in the house of the Lord.

True prophetic ministry will only destroy what is of the devil; it will never destroy what is of the Lord.

We don't need more church members who are not rooted and planted. We need saints who are planted in the house by the Lord. Those who are planted will develop strong roots, and they will be like trees planted by the rivers of living water. The planting of the Lord will be fruitful Christians who will be steadfast, unmovable, and always abounding in the work of the Lord (1 Cor. 15:58). As we receive prophetic ministry, we will become trees of righteousness, the planting of the Lord (Isa. 61:3).

I am firmly convinced that one of the reasons we don't have more fruitful Christians in our local assemblies is because of the lack of true prophetic ministry. I have been ministering and telling people for years that it takes the anointing to perfect the saints. Each ministry gift carries a distinct anointing. Each ministry gift has a divine ability to build the church. Prophets have an anointing and ability to build and to plant. Without this anointing, there will be areas where the saints are not built up and things they are not planted in.

To summarize, prophets have the authority from God to *root out*, to *pull down*, to *destroy*, to *throw down*, to *build*, and to *plant*. These will be the identifiable results of the word of the Lord that comes out of the mouths of the prophets.

GETTING IN THE FLOW

Prophets must never use their authority to control or abuse God's people. Control and domination are forms of witchcraft. To insure against the abuse of their authority, prophets must work to develop godly character, and they must walk in humility.

Prophets can also work together in teams. Teams help keep prophets balanced, and teamwork provides a healthy barrier against pride, isolation, and exclusiveness. We have many recognized prophets in our local assembly, and they understand that teamwork is the way to go.

We need to be connected with people who flow strongly in prophetic ministry. When you move in the prophetic, a whole new realm of authority and spiritual ability opens up to you. You can move in prophetic music, which includes playing prophetically, singing prophetic songs, and singing new songs. You need to be able to get in the flow.

> He sendeth out his word, and melteth them: he causeth his wind to blow, and the waters flow.
>
> —PSALM 147:18

When you are in the flow, you will prophesy not only to other saints. You will also begin prophesying unto God and unto principalities and powers. You can prophesy to devils and kingdoms in the spirit realm. This is how the tearing down of strongholds happens. The prophet Jeremiah was anointed of God to prophesy to kingdoms and nations. He had authority to tear down kingdoms and to exercise rule over nations.

One of the reasons why we don't have more fruitful Christians in our local assemblies is because of the lack of true prophetic ministry.

According to 1 Corinthians 2:10, the Spirit searches the deep things of God. The twelfth verse goes on to say that we have been given the Spirit of God that we might know the things that are freely given to us of God. So prophesying to God is speaking to Him out of your spirit according to the depths of revelation that the Spirit of God has given you.

God already knows what He is going to do. The problem comes when God has to have someone on the earth fulfill His plan. There can be things in the heavenlies that God wants to do. God knows about it, for He has decreed it. Jesus, the Holy Ghost, and the angels are all aware of it. All heaven is in one accord, but it is different when God tries to get it established in the realm of the earth.

When you begin to prophesy out of your spirit, that is God flowing out of you. Whatever is bound in heaven is bound on the earth. Whatever God establishes in heaven and makes to flow out of us on the earth, that is exactly what is going to be established in the earth's realm.

One of the prayers we pray goes like this: "Thy kingdom come. Thy will be done in earth, as it is in heaven" (Matt. 6:10). It is the God in heaven who is in you, speaking out of you on the earth, joining heaven to the earth. He desires to fulfill His plan in the earth's realm that we might walk and live in His will. We are not trying to be God. We are just His instruments. We know that without God, we can do nothing.

Most of us have never really understood the authority that we have in the prophetic realm. We think we are very different from the great prophets of old who walked in tremendous authority. Joshua had the authority to stop the heavenly motion, to stop the moon and the sun. Moses walked in enough authority to open a pathway in the Red Sea. These men of God knew how to flow in the prophetic realm.

Most of God's people, most churches, don't know how to flow in that type of authority. That is why we sit around twiddling our thumbs, waiting for God to perform everything automatically. Just imagine Moses standing on the shore of the Red Sea, with the Egyptian army bearing down on the Israelites, just "waiting on God to do something." That would have been the end of the story right then and there; they all would have died.

Many times God is waiting on us to flow with Him. His anointing, initiative, and power are there for us, but since most of us have not been taught how, we do not know how to flow in the prophetic. I have found that often, in a conference, it is very difficult to break through in prophetic songs because there are so many religious people in the service who don't know how to flow prophetically. When I get up to prophesy or to give a message in tongues, they are jumping, singing, and clapping because they have never been taught how to flow in the anointing. Their actions are not wrong, but they are misplaced, and they throw off the entire service. The whole church needs to learn how to flow with the anointing.

> Behold, how good and how pleasant it is for brethren to dwell together in unity!
>
> —PSALM 133:1

Anointing flows from the head down

If you want a prophetic church, you must have prophetic leadership, because the anointing always flows from the head down. In the Book of Psalms, the Bible reports that when Aaron was anointed, the oil flowed from his head all the way down to the skirts of his garments. The anointing always flows down. It doesn't flow up.

If the leadership of a local assembly does not flow in the prophetic anointing, then the people are not going to flow in prophecy. If the leadership does not flow in miracles, the congregation will not flow in miracles. That is why it is futile for people who get a hold of something at a conference to think they are going to take it back and transform their churches with it. Unless they are church leaders themselves, they will be trying to get the anointing to flow upward.

I don't care how much you know about deliverance or prophecy; if you try to introduce it into your church instead of the leaders doing it, you are going to end up getting hurt and disappointed. You will waste years trying to create a spiritual move in that church, but it will not work, because you do not have the authority—unless you get into a prophetic realm of praying and you pray it in.

You have to get into the authority in the spirit world in order to bring things into manifestation in your local church. God will then put it on the heart of your pastor, and it will flow down under the authority of that pastor. Any other move in a church is a rebellious uprising, and God cannot bless it.

> And the LORD came down in a cloud, and spake unto him, and took of the spirit that was upon him, and gave it unto the seventy elders: and it came to pass, that, when the spirit rested upon them, they prophesied, and did not cease.
> —NUMBERS 11:25

God wants a prophetic people, and He is looking for people who will flow in miracles. But you will never flow in miracles in advance of your leadership. When your leadership begins to flow in miracles, that anointing will flow down upon everyone under their authority. It always works that way.

If you want a prophetic church, you must have prophetic leadership, because the anointing always flows from the head down.

That's why you can go to some churches and if the leadership is not flowing in the prophetic, chances are, there is not going to be much prophesying, no matter how much you want to flow in the prophetic. There are not going to be very many new songs birthed, even though you personally may be able to flow in that anointing.

I know you can minister to laypeople all day long, but unless the leadership is ahead of them, the church is not going to be effective to the degree that God desires. It is because the leaders are keeping the people out of that realm. Remember, you just cannot go beyond your leadership.

For this reason, my heart is set on those in leadership. This is why I try to reach pastors and leaders. It is so important to minister to them first. Whether or not you are a leader, pray for church leadership. God is raising up prophetic leaders, people of authority, people who will be able to flow in miracles. They are going to minister, and when they do, the anointing is going to come down upon the people of God to the extent that they follow their leaders into different realms of the Spirit of God.

chapter five

PROPHETS WHO PROTECT

THE CHURCH HAS often assumed that pastors are the spiritual guardians of the church, while neglecting the ministry of prophets. However, the church was never intended to function with only pastors serving as protectors of the people. Prophets also have been set in the church to help fulfill this important role (1 Cor. 12:28). Churches that ignore this aspect of the prophetic ministry will not be able to withstand the attacks of hell in the last days.

Hosea 12:13 reveals to us that one of the major functions of the prophet's ministry is preservation:

> And by a prophet the LORD brought Israel out of Egypt,
> and by a prophet was he preserved.

Israel was delivered from Egypt through the ministry of the prophet Moses, and then Israel was preserved through the intercession of Moses (Num. 14:11–20).

The word *preserve* means to keep from harm, damage, danger, or evil. It also means to protect or to save. In Hebrew, the root word is *shamar*. *Shamar* means to hedge about (as with thorns), to guard, to protect, to watch, and to keep. The word *shamar* is first used in Scripture in Genesis 2:15, where Adam is told to keep (*shamar*) the garden. It is also mentioned in Genesis 4:9, where Cain asks God if he is his brother's keeper (*shamar*).

SHAMAR

This word *shamar* emphasizes the protective element of the prophet's mantle. The preserving and guarding aspect of the prophet's ministry is needed in every local church. Many well-meaning pastors have suffered unnecessarily due to the lack of understanding this aspect of the ministry of the prophet. The shamar aspect of the prophet's ministry is one of the most important ones, and it will benefit the church greatly.

The local church is kept safe through prophetic intercession, prophetic discernment, prophetic praise, prophetic preaching, prophetic teaching, and prophetic worship. This is how the church is best defended. Without a revelation of the shamar aspect of the prophetic ministry, a local church will suffer from many attacks that can be averted.

Each church should identify, develop, and train the shamar prophets who have been set in their assembly by God. A revelation of the importance of the ministry of shamar prophets is vital to the success and long-term health of every church. Because the role of shamar prophets is so important, I will devote most of this chapter and the next one to an explanation of how they can help pastors of churches protect and defend their flocks.

Watchman

Shamar means to guard, to keep, to be a watchman. It can refer to guarding a flock, the heart, the mind, a nation, or a city from outside attack or ungodly influences. It is used in reference to keeping (guarding) the gates or entries to cities. Each local church needs a prophetic guard. This is not one prophet but a company of prophets who help guard the church from the invasion of the enemy. Churches that develop the prophetic ministry will have the advantage of being protected through prophetic intercession and the shamar aspect of the prophetic ministry.

To *guard* means a number of things. It can mean to protect, to watch over, to stand guard over, to police, to secure, to defend, to shield, to shelter, to screen, to cover, to cloak, to preserve, to save, to conserve, to supervise, to keep under surveillance or control, to keep under guard, to govern, to restrain, to suppress, to keep watch, to be alert, or to take care. Synonyms for *guard* include protector, defender, guardian, custodian, watchman, sentinel, sentry, patrol, and garrison. These words help us visualize and define the shamar aspect of the prophetic ministry.

Without a revelation of the shamar aspect of the prophetic ministry, a local church will suffer from many attacks that can be averted.

The shamar components of the prophetic mantle pertain to the prophet's role as a guardian tending to the flock over which he or she has care. It applies to the guardian function of the office, the aspect of prophetic ministry that makes a person like a sentinel or a protector. To shamar a people is to work prophetically, to encircle the people or the church with a divine wall or hedge of protection—or to reseal the gap in the hedge through which the devil has broken in with satanic assaults, attacks, and warfare.

Look at these examples from the Bible that use the word *shamar*:

> Except the LORD build the house, they labour in vain that build it: except the LORD keep the city, the watchman waketh but in vain.
>
> —PSALM 127:1

> My soul waiteth for the Lord more than they that watch for the morning: I say, more than they that watch for the morning.
>
> —PSALM 130:6

> I have set watchmen upon thy walls, O Jerusalem, which shall never hold their peace day nor night: ye that make mention of the LORD, keep not silence.
>
> —ISAIAH 62:6

> The watchmen that go about the city found me: to whom I said, Saw ye him whom my soul loveth?
>
> —SONG OF SOLOMON 3:3

We can see that watchmen duties in the church are accomplished through the prayer, intercessions, and petitions of the prophet on behalf of the local body of believers. Such a guard would consist of the prayer team, the special intercessors, dedicated psalmists, seers, and subordinate prophets. It is the word *shamar* that emphasizes the status of prophets as spiritual guards, warriors, supernatural enforcers, and keepers of the churches of God. Without the help of the watchmen, pastors cannot take care of their flocks. As a result, the people of God become open prey to the enemy forces:

My people hath been lost sheep: their shepherds have caused them to go astray, they have turned them away on the mountains: they have gone from mountain to hill, they have forgotten their restingplace. All that found them have devoured them: and their adversaries said, We offend not.

—JEREMIAH 50:6–7

Building a hedge of protection

Additionally, the word *shamar* identifies a prophet who encircles (or surrounds) to retain and attend to, as one does a garden. The prophet's spiritual authority acts as a fence or garrison around an assigned congregation to shield it from harm, attack, or demonic trespass. Protection from trespassers, as meant here, includes protection from the spoilage, destruction, invasion, and threats that result from spiritual and human trespassers in the church.

Behold, he that keepeth [*shamar*] Israel shall neither slumber nor sleep. The LORD is thy keeper [*shamar*]: the LORD is thy shade upon thy right hand. The sun shall not smite thee by day, nor the moon by night. The LORD shall preserve [*shamar*] thee from all evil: he shall preserve [*shamar*] thy soul. The LORD shall preserve [*shamar*] thy going out and thy coming in from this time forth, and even for evermore.

—PSALM 121:4–8

We can see from these verses that God shamars His people. God loves His people and protects them. The shamar aspect of the prophet's ministry is a part of the nature of God. God never slumbers or sleeps. He is always alert. God shamars us from evil. God shamars our souls (our minds, wills, and emotions). God shamars

71

our going out and coming in (our travels). It is the nature of God to protect. Protection from God is a part of our covenant with Him, and shamar prophets are therefore a practical part of the working out of our covenant relationship with God.

Role and position

There are times when heretical types or wayward renegades join a church to sow seeds of destruction in it. The watchful eye of the resident prophet can spot these people and bring spiritual discomfort on them so they are ill at ease among the flock and quickly leave.

Shamar means to guard, to keep, to be a watchman.

Some leaders look at prophets as translocal ministries only; in their view only the pastor's role is stationary. Of course, it is always a blessing to bring prophets in from the outside to minister to a congregation. But this does not replace prophets who are stationed in the house, shamar prophets who are a part of the local church, just as a pastor is.

Prophets need an understanding of their role and position in the local church. Having a revelation of the shamar aspect of their prophet's mantle will help them to fulfill their ministries more fully.

The shamar aspect of the prophet's ministry can also be seen in the life of Samuel:

> So the Philistines were subdued, and they came no more into the coast of Israel: and *the hand of the LORD was against the Philistines all the days of Samuel.*
> —1 SAMUEL 7:13, emphasis added

The Philistines were subdued and could not enter the coasts of Israel as long as Samuel was alive. This gives us a good picture of the power of a prophet's presence.

The enemy hates the prophet because the prophet's presence thwarts his advances. This is why he has done everything in his power to keep prophets from being recognized and operational in the church, and his efforts are often visible if we look for self-limiting unbelief, fear, or tradition.

MANIFESTATIONS OF ENEMY ADVANCES

We can rejoice that we live in a day when we are currently seeing the restoration of the prophetic ministry and a corresponding release of revelation and understanding concerning this ministry.

Shamar prophets help guard the church against:

- Accusation
- Apathy
- Backbiting
- Backsliding
- Betrayal
- Carnality
- Compromise
- Confusion
- Control
- Covetousness
- Death
- Deception
- Destruction
- Disorder
- Division
- Doctrines of devils

- False prophets, apostles, and teachers
- False teaching
- Financial attacks
- Gossip
- Greed
- Idolatry
- Immorality
- Jealousy
- Jezebel
- Legalism
- Lukewarmness
- Pride
- Rebellion
- Sickness
- Slander
- Slothfulness
- Strife
- Treachery
- Witchcraft

In addition to identifying these potential enemies, shamar prophets ought to seek God so that they can develop strategies to resist, expel, and overcome them in the power of the Holy Ghost. These strategies can include prayer, fasting, worshiping, teaching, preaching, correcting, and outright expelling. In other words, prophets should do more than cry, "Thus saith the Lord." That will not be adequate. As a defense, it is insufficient. Shamar prophets are a part of the covenant community and have a vested interest in the health of the flock. They are not outsiders looking in. They must love the church. They must experience the joy of victory and the grief of the enemies' attacks on the saints they love. Jeremiah wept for Israel because he was a part of Israel and suffered with Israel. Prophets must understand that God has "set" them in the church, which means that they have been appointed, established, or positioned in this role.

Each church should identify, develop, and train the shamar prophets who have been set in their assembly by God.

Shamar prophets help protect the preaching, teaching, evangelism, worship, and intercession of the local church. They help identify and confront religious spirits, occult spirits, spirits of sin, pride, rebellion, and witchcraft.

Shamar prophets are the spiritual immune system of a local church. They help fight off spiritual disease that is Satan's effort to undermine the health of the church. Shamar prophets are needed for the overall health of the church.

Shamar prophets help to protect the vision of the church. They also help to confirm the vision of the church. They help ward off Satan's attack on the vision of the church. They must share a divine jealousy for the health of the church and the purposes of God for the church. (See 2 Corinthians 11.)

Problems that can occur without the shamar anointing

Sometimes it is not enough to talk only about what "should be." Often we only become convinced of a need when we look at the compelling needs around us. In a local assembly, problems such as the following reveal the gaping holes in the defenses of the church. Without an operational shamar anointing, these problems are all too common:

- Accidents
- Apathy
- Attacks on the pastor and the family
- Backsliding
- Broken relationships
- Church splits
- Confusion
- Conspiracies
- Control and domination
- Divorces and separations
- Failures in leadership
- False brethren
- False prophets, false teachers, false apostles
- False teaching, error, or heresy
- Family problems
- Financial setbacks
- Hindrances, blockages, or obstructions
- Immorality
- Infighting and division
- Loss of anointing
- Manipulation
- Occultists
- People leaving the church
- Premature deaths
- Satanists
- Stagnation
- Unexplainable sicknesses and illnesses
- Warlocks
- Witches
- Wolves entering the flock

SPIRITS TO WAR AGAINST

There are certain spirits that will attack congregations. These spirits seem to specialize in undermining the body of Christ in every locality. Over time, the church has given them biblical names to better identify them and resist them.

The Jezebel spirit

> Notwithstanding I have a few things against thee, because thou sufferest that woman Jezebel, which calleth herself a prophetess, to teach and to seduce my servants to commit fornication, and to eat things sacrificed unto idols.
> —REVELATION 2:20

The prophet Elijah warred against Jezebel. God raised up Elijah during the time Jezebel was destroying the nation through idolatry and witchcraft. The Jezebel spirit will always seek to destroy and hinder the development of the prophetic ministry in a church. Jezebel will attempt to kill true prophets. The Jezebel spirit operates through members of a congregation. The Jezebel spirit is responsible for false prophecies. This spirit operates through divination, control, manipulation, and domination. Jezebel is also responsible for false teaching and sexual impurity.

Shamar prophets are the spiritual immune system of a local church.

Jezebel spirits have destroyed many congregations. Many leaders have fallen victim to Jezebel because Jezebel loves to be in a position of leadership. The spirit will gain influence by inciting slander and gossip to harm the ordained leaders of the church. Jezebel hates ordained leadership and will do everything possible to destroy it or control it. (Athaliah, the daughter of Jezebel, attempted to kill the royal seed [2 Kings 11:1]).

Jim Goll has stated that "a Jezebel spirit stirs up fear, flight, and discouragement, often prompting a spiritual leader to flee his or her appointed place just as Elijah did. Every year hundreds of spiritual marketplace and governmental leaders resign because of debilitating discouragement, confusion, depression, loss of vision, despair, disorientation, withdrawal, a sense of worthlessness, defeat, burnout, physical illness, financial insufficiency, character assassination, moral failure, and an almost infinite variety of other factors. In many cases, this maligning control spirit is responsible."[1]

The Jezebel spirit hates prophets because they are her greatest threat. Jezebel will attempt to cut off intercession. Jezebel will attack the prayer ministry of a church. In the biblical event, Jezebel was able to gain power and influence over Israel through her marriage to King Ahab. Marriage is a covenant, and this marriage covenant gave Jezebel the legal right to enter Israel, bringing with her all of her idolatry, witchcraft, and whoredom.

This should warn us that leaders must be very careful whom they enter into covenant with. One wrong covenant can open the door for a Jezebel.

Prophets walk in discernment and can detect Jezebel. Even before a Jezebel spirit is evident to them, prophets should pray for the leaders of the church. They must provide a prayer covering to prevent Jezebel from gaining influence.

Just as Ahab's wife Jezebel was notorious for being very manipulative, so is the Jezebel spirit. Prophets can discern and expose subtle manipulation through teaching, false prophecy, and flattery. The influence of the Jezebel spirit will always be seen in false teaching and efforts to control decisions. It may also involve witchcraft, seduction, and sexual sin. Obviously, a church cannot remain healthy with the influence of a seducing Jezebel spirit. This spirit seduces believers, leading them astray, misleading them.

The Jezebel spirit causes churches to be guided more by the flesh than by the Spirit. The spirit of Jezebel draws the whole church away from purity and interferes with true worship. When a Jezebel spirit is present, spirits of perversion, adultery, immorality, and fornication will run rampant in a body of people. Slander and gossip are the marks of this spirit.

Churches under the influence of a Jezebel spirit will go astray in their doctrine. Dangerous false teaching and heresy will affect the lifestyles of the saints, and even once-strong assemblies will find themselves in a broken-down, weakened condition. The Jezebel spirit is like a black widow spider, which is deadly and will even eat its mate. (The name Jezebel means "unhusbanded.")

John Paul Jackson states, "No church is too great, too healthy, or too pure to be exempted from an attack by a Jezebel spirit. In fact, the greater the church, the greater the assurance that those with a Jezebel spirit will seek to gain influence and power—unless the pastor, the leadership team, the intercessors, and prophetically gifted individuals exercise their responsibility and withstand this spiritual attack."[2]

The Absalom spirit

> And Absalom rose up early, and stood beside the way of the gate....so Absalom stole the hearts of the men of Israel....And the conspiracy was strong; for the people increased continually with Absalom.
>
> —2 SAMUEL 15:2, 6, 12

Absalom rebelled against his father, David, and tried to seize the kingdom. In other words, he was disloyal to his father, and he acted out of pride, vanity, rebellion, and bitterness.

Therefore, an Absalom spirit represents betrayal and treachery. Many leaders have suffered betrayal and treachery from other leaders who have Absalom spirits, resulting in splits and defections. Prophets need to be on guard against this spirit that seeks to divide and separate churches.

Absalom turned the hearts of the people away from David, who was the rightful king. Absalom tried to usurp his authority by gaining followers. Even Ahithophel, David's wisest counselor, joined the rebellion. In a similar way, many leaders have suffered betrayal from people with Absalom spirits.

The shamar anointing is designed to see hidden conspiracies and expose them before it is too late.

The Absalom spirit can be stopped through prophetic intercession. It is interesting to note that Absalom stood by "the way of the gate" to seduce the people into becoming his followers. This proves the importance of having prophetic intercession at the gates of the church. (We will talk more about this in the next chapter.)

David almost lost his throne to Absalom. He had to flee Jerusalem for his life. He had been unaware of what Absalom was doing beforehand. Absalom planned a conspiracy against his father, David. He planned and acted together secretly with others who were not happy with the way things were going under David's leadership. The conspiracy continued to gain strength as the number of people increased who went to Absalom's side. An Absalom spirit will attempt to get as many people on its side—against leadership—as possible. Subtle and cunning, an Absalom spirit will carry out its rebellion secretly. Ambitious, subtle, and crafty, this spirit will go after the father figure or leader. Sometimes the Absalom spirit will attack the spiritual sons and daughters of a leader. The Absalom spirit is like a serpent, sliding in between people to attack them.

Many leaders have fallen victim to ungodly conspiracies perpetrated by other leaders in the church. These hidden plots came as a surprise. Too often, even when leaders try to recover, it is too late. Hidden conspiracies have not been exposed soon enough.

The shamar anointing is designed to see hidden conspiracies and expose them before it is too late.

The Korah spirit

> Now Korah, the son of Izhar, the son of Kohath, the son of Levi, and Dathan and Abiram, the sons of Eliab, and On, the son of Peleth, sons of Reuben, took men: and they rose up before Moses, with certain of the children of Israel, two hundred and fifty princes of the assembly, famous in the congregation, men of renown: and they gathered themselves together against Moses and against Aaron.
> —Numbers 16:1–3

Korah also represents rebellion, although he was more open and defiant than Absalom. Korah openly challenged the leadership of Moses and Aaron. Korah accused Moses of exalting himself above the other leaders. The insinuation was that he was holding the other leaders down. Whereas the Jezebel spirit seems to work primarily through women, the Korah spirit seems to work primarily through men.

As we know, rebellion is as the sin of witchcraft (1 Sam. 15:23). Witchcraft operates through all three of these evil spirits: Jezebel,

Absalom, and Korah. If unchecked, witchcraft can blind and seduce many believers in a congregation.

The Korah spirit will cause a leader to exalt himself in the midst of the congregation, disregarding God's appointed leadership. The Korah spirit is bold and brazen, not afraid to speak openly against leadership. This spirit accuses leaders of being self-appointed instead of God appointed.

The devil hates God's ordained leaders, and he will attempt to slander, pull down, accuse, and overthrow those who have been ordained to be leaders. The Korah spirit is one of those spirits that attempt to exalt a person to challenge true leadership. The Korah spirit hates apostolic and prophetic leadership.

Prophets must stand alongside the leadership of the church against the spirit of Korah, which will appear as a spirit of revolt, a refusal to submit to established authority.

The python spirit

> And it came to pass, as we went to prayer, a certain damsel possessed with a spirit of divination [python] met us.
> —ACTS 16:16

The word *python* is translated here as divination, and a python is a constrictor snake. Pythons kill their victims by squeezing the breath out of them, and the breath represents the spirit of a person. Python spirits attempt to choke the life out of churches. This can include choking the life out of the praise and worship and the prophetic ministry. Python spirits also attempt to squeeze the prayer life out of the church. (Remember, the damsel possessed with the spirit of python met the apostles as they were going to prayer.)

People with python spirits will attempt to stop or constrict the move of the Holy Spirit in the church. The evil spirit will try to curtail the new life that the Spirit of God brings. This spirit convinces leaders to draw back from the gifts of the Spirit and a move of the Holy Ghost. When any spirit attempts to stop the flow of the Holy Spirit or pervert it, we call it "witchcraft."

The noticeable characteristics of a church that is affected by a python spirit can include a lack of prophecy and other manifestations of the Holy Spirit, prayerlessness, tiredness and spiritual lethargy, lack of fervent praise and worship, and lack of development of ministries. False gifts and manifestations can occur instead of genuine manifestations of the Holy Spirit. Churches should experience a continual flow and anointing of the Holy Spirit. Something is seriously wrong when the spiritual life is getting choked out of the church.

Prophets are sensitive to the operations of the Holy Spirit, and they have the ability to sense when something is wrong. They not only sense something is wrong, but they can also identify the problem. Prophetic intercession can stop witchcraft and divination from entering and affecting the spiritual flow of a congregation.

The Leviathan spirit

> In that day the LORD with his sore and great and strong sword shall punish leviathan the piercing serpent, even leviathan that crooked serpent; and he shall slay the dragon that is in the sea.
>
> —ISAIAH 27:1

Leviathan is the king over all the children of pride. The Leviathan spirit, represented by a crocodile or a large sea serpent, attacks leaders, causing them to become arrogant and puffed up. We are aware that

God resists the proud but gives grace to the humble (1 Pet. 5:5) and that humility is a prerequisite for accessing the grace of God.

The most extensive reference to Leviathan is found in chapter 41 of the Book of Job. Accordingly, the characteristics of the Leviathan spirit include prayerlessness (Job 41:3), harsh words (v. 3), covenant breaking (v. 4), an inability to serve others (v. 4), no breath (or spirit, or air; v. 16), stubbornness (or being stiff-necked; v. 24), hardness of heart (v. 24), and, above all, pride (v. 34). Pride opens the door for destruction (Prov. 16:18).

Ministries can become proud through knowledge and success (1 Cor. 8:1), but this is the opposite of humility, which is the key to honor and success. A lack of humility will open the doors for spirits of pride, arrogance, haughtiness, and self-exaltation. These are dangerous spirits that must be identified and driven out and away from the assembly.

Prophetic Protection

Prophetic intercession—divinely inspired prayers that target evil influences and take them out—is one of the primary functions of a shamar prophet.

Each area of a church should be covered by the prophet's intercession. This includes the following:

- The pastor (apostle, set man)
- The elders (presbytery, bishops)
- The prophets and prophetic teams, intercessors
- The praise and worship teams (minstrels and psalmists)
- The deacons
- The pastors (shepherds)
- The teachers (doctors, instructors)

- The evangelists and evangelistic teams
- The helps ministry
- The administrators (governments)
- The dance teams
- The youth ministry
- The children's ministry
- The business ministry
- The finances
- The missions (nations)
- The media outreach (television and radio)
- The new believers
- The new members
- Married couples
- Singles
- Men and women
- Widows
- Families

Prophetic intercession also includes prayer for the release of:

- Church growth
- Deliverance
- Evangelism
- Favor
- Gifts of the Holy Spirit
- Glory
- Healing
- Holiness
- Humility
- Love
- Miracles

- Peace
- Property
- Prophecy
- Prophetic worship
- Prosperity
- Protecting angels
- Revelation
- Salvation
- Signs and wonders
- Strength
- Unity
- Wisdom

We will continue this discussion of prophetic protection in the next chapter.

chapter six

PROPHETS AT THE GATES

I<small>N THE</small> B<small>IBLE</small>, watchmen were positioned at the outer defenses (the wall of a city or the hedge fence of a field) or in a raised outlook or tower that overlooked the territory that needed to be watched. A watchman is one who stands guard. Ancient cities had watchmen stationed on the walls. Their responsibility was to sound a warning if an enemy approached. (See 2 Kings 9:17; Ezekiel 33:2–3.) The Israelites also posed watchmen to serve as sentinels over their vineyards and fields, especially during harvest. Their responsibility was to guard the produce from animals and thieves. In a similar way, Israel's prophets saw themselves as watchmen, warning the nation of God's approaching judgment if the people did not repent.

Today, one way of identifying their position and role is to say that the watchmen guard the *gates*—of a local church and more. If you read Scripture with the word *gates* in mind, you begin to see this connection everywhere. For example, consider the following passages from the Old Testament:

And it shall come to pass, that thy choicest valleys shall be full of chariots, and the horsemen shall set themselves in array at the *gate*.
—ISAIAH 22:7, emphasis added

For he hath strengthened the bars of thy *gates*; he hath blessed thy children within thee. He maketh peace in thy borders, and filleth thee with the finest of the wheat.
—PSALM 147:13–14, emphasis added

...then was war in the *gates*...
—JUDGES 5:8, emphasis added

Then Daniel requested of the king, and he set Shadrach, Meshach, and Abed-nego, over the affairs of the province of Babylon: but Daniel sat in the *gate* of the king.
—DANIEL 2:49, emphasis added

Gates are entry points, and they need to be strengthened in order to keep the enemy out and to keep the people and all that they possess safe. The prophet's ministry helps strengthen the gates so that the children will be blessed and peace will be within the church. With the benefit of the protection of the prophetic ministry, the church will be filled with the finest of the wheat (prosperity).

The watchmen guard the gates—of a local church and more.

People who serve in the office of the prophet need to have an understanding of gates and entry points in their churches, their cities, their regions, and their nations. Having a revelation of gates and their importance will help prophets defend these entry points from invasion by the enemy. When prophets gain a clearer understanding of their role and position in the church, a revelation of the shamar aspect of the prophet's mantle, they will be better able to fulfill their ministries.

Praise is a gate

Praise is a gate (Isa. 60:18). That is why the enemy often attempts to attack and infiltrate the praise and worship of a church. He attacks praise leaders, minstrels, and psalmists. Prophets must help protect this gate through intercession. (See Psalm 118:19–20.)

Prophets can speak with the enemies in the gate (Ps. 127:5). *Speak* is the Hebrew word *dabar,* which can mean to command, to subdue, or to warn. To be as effective as possible as watchmen at the gates of the church, it is important that prophets, those who sit in the gate, keep themselves from speaking evil against the leadership of the church. (See Psalm 69:12.)

Prophets in leadership

If the enemy is victorious in the gates, the church is in trouble. This is why prophets must be a part of the leadership of the local church. They have been set into the church "second" by God:

> And God hath set some in the church, first apostles, secondarily prophets, thirdly teachers, after that miracles, then gifts of healings, helps, governments, diversities of tongues.
>
> —1 Corinthians 12:28

Prophets should be a part of the music ministry, the youth ministry, the children's ministry, the presbytery, and the overall ministry of a church. Each ministry represents a specific gate, and each gate of a church needs prophetic intercession. Prophets will intercede and stop the enemy at the gates. They will go to war against demons in the gates where they have been stationed.

The warfare will always be at the gates because that is where the defenders clash with the invading enemies. The enemies "set themselves in array" at the gate. That is where demons launch their attacks. This is why we need prophets standing watch at the gates.

Not only are prophets assigned by God to the numerous gates of a local church, but there are also "gateway churches" (in other words, apostolic churches) that are the key to a region or territory. These gateway churches need highly qualified prophets to keep the enemy out. Strong prophetic intercession is a must if the gates are to be protected.

Preventing destruction

A church will lose its protection if the gates are destroyed. The destruction of a gate results in unwanted things entering in. Demons can enter a church and establish strongholds if the gates are open. A destroyed gate means that nothing can be closed. "In the city desolation is left, and the gate is stricken with destruction" (Isa. 24:12, NKJV).

The gate represents a place of authority, and the enemy wants to unseat that authority so that he can plunder the inhabitants and usurp the authority for himself. The inhabitants cannot effectively counter the enemy's advance unless their defenses are coordinated by someone with the proper authority to do so. The prophet has the spiritual authority to stand at the gate and challenge the enemy. When demons attack the gates and attempt to destroy them, they cannot get past the prophets who stand strong at the gates, alert and well fortified with the anointing of God.

Rebuke in the gates

The gate is a place where the enemy can be rebuked. To *rebuke* means to force back. A rebuke is a sharp reprimand. A reprimand is a severe or formal rebuke by a person in authority.

Each ministry represents a specific gate, and each gate of a church needs prophetic intercession.

Demons need to be rebuked. They need to be beaten back. Prophetic intercession rebukes the enemy, and it takes place in the gates, the very centers of traffic and business in every area of the kingdom of God. Spirits of witchcraft, lust, rebellion, deception, pride, Jezebel, religion, and carnality must be rebuked in the gates. This will prevent them from entering in and destroying the church.

Needless to say, demonic spirits do not yield quietly to rebuke. They will resist and struggle. They hate the gatekeepers, the prophetic watchmen who interfere with their evil plans:

> They hate him that rebuketh in the gate.
>
> —Amos 5:10

A word of prevention

Often a prophet will be able to warn a leader about an encroaching enemy, and the warning will prevent a disaster. Sometimes, the best defense is simple prevention.

> But Elisha, the prophet that is in Israel, telleth the king of Israel the words that thou speakest in thy bedchamber.
>
> —2 Kings 6:12

Elisha was able to warn the king and prevent him from being ambushed. The prophet's ministry is preventive. It is better to prevent something from happening than having to react to it after it happens.

The vineyard of God

Besides being like a walled city with gates at intervals in the protective wall, the church is God's vineyard.

The church is a divine institution ordained by God and hated by the enemy. The church is the Israel of God, and He Himself has set up its defenses:

> Now will I sing to my wellbeloved a song of my beloved touching his vineyard. My wellbeloved hath a vineyard in a very fruitful hill: And he *fenced it*, and gathered out the stones thereof, and planted it with the choicest vine, and *built a tower* in the midst of it, and also made a winepress therein.
>
> —ISAIAH 5:1–2, emphasis added

Israel is God's vineyard, and so is the church. The result of the planting of the Lord should be fruitfulness. We have been ordained to bring forth fruit and for the fruit to remain (John 15:16). But the enemy wants to destroy the fruit of churches and ministries. There-fore, the local church needs prophets to prevent the fruit from being destroyed.

It is unwise to plant a vineyard without a fence. A fence provides a protective barrier for the vineyard. A tower is a place for the watchman. The Lord hedges His vineyard. He places a tower in the midst. These are both pictures of the prophet's ministry in the church. The hedge and the tower are necessary to keep the enemy out.

Vineyards need watchmen too, just as cities do. It is just a different picture of what local churches need—towers and watchmen and gatekeepers to protect the life of God's people.

The gate is a place where the enemy can be rebuked.

Now, the enemy plots to destroy the tree with its fruit. He spends all of his effort devising devices:

> I knew not that they had devised devices against me, saying, Let us destroy the tree with the fruit thereof.
>
> —JEREMIAH 11:19

Devise is the Hebrew word *chashab*, meaning to plait or to weave. Another word for it is *impenetrate*, which is related to the word *impenetrable*. Something that is impenetrable cannot be solved or understood. To *plait* means to braid or interweave, and to *interweave* means to connect closely or intricately. In other words, the enemy sets up intricate plans against the church. It takes a prophet's anointing to unweave these plots.

THE PROPHET'S WARD

> My lord, I stand continually upon the watchtower in the daytime, and I am set *in my ward* whole nights.
>
> —ISAIAH 21:8, emphasis added

Ward is an interesting word. In Hebrew it is the word *mishmereth*, meaning watch, the sentry, the post, preservation, office, ordinance, a safeguard. It is from the root word *mishmar*, meaning a guard.

The prophet Isaiah was set in his ward. *Set* is the word *natsab*, meaning to station, a pillar. Since a ward is a means of defense or protection and *ward* is the root of the word *warden*, and since a warden is a person who guards or has charge of something, prophets are spiritual wardens. They have been set into particular, assigned positions, and they help guard and protect the house of the Lord from the enemy. Many local churches have been defenseless against the enemy because they do not have prophets stationed in their wards.

Not only must local churches have prophetic wards established to preserve the church from the attacks of the devil, but also the prophets must station themselves in their respective wards like spiritual superintendents. They must watch and pray to fortify the church, protecting the church from spiritual infiltration.

The prophet was set in his ward whole nights. I believe this can be a reference to all-night prayer being an effective way of preventing the enemy from infiltrating the church.

A tower is a place for the watchman.

Prophets are appointed and set in their wards by God. They are responsible to take their place as watchmen and protect the church. They must stand continually upon the watchtower. They must be faithful to their assigned posts. They cannot vacate their wards. They must understand their importance to the safety and protection of the church.

They must set themselves in a posture of prayer and intercession. They must not move from their set position. Satan will attempt to cause prophets to move out of their places. He will attempt to discourage them and prevent them from taking their places in the watchtower in the first place. For their part, prophets must take on an attitude of being unmovable. They must accept their assignments, stand in their assigned places, and fulfill their ministries.

Prophets should ask, "Where is my ward?" and when they find out, they will know that God has placed them there. They must have a revelation of their assigned position. Then they must set themselves in that place and *watch*, operating as spiritual wardens to protect those over whom they have been given charge. Prophets have been assigned as spiritual wardens in many situations, from local churches, to cities, to regions, to nations.

Seeing and saying

After watchmen have been set, they are responsible to declare what they see:

> For thus hath the Lord said unto me, Go, set a watchman,
> let him declare what he seeth.
>
> —Isaiah 21:6

Shamar prophets, or watchmen prophets, have been set or put into their proper or designated places, *and these are the places* in which they will have the strongest ability to see with spiritual vision. They will be able to see with spiritual eyes that can penetrate the impenetrable. They will be able to see what others cannot see. And they will be able to *say* what they see.

They will make declarations and reveal hidden things. They will pray decisive prayers that will keep their set charge, whether it be a ministry, a church, a city, a region, or a nation, safe and flourishing.

In the Old Testament, prophets were called seers, and they are still seers today. Every local church needs seer watchmen.

From earliest times, watchman prophets have helped prevent the enemy from destroying the people of God and their property. Many things can be prevented through the watchman prophet's ministry. It is the will of God that many things be prevented. Everything that happens is not necessarily the will of God. Prophets help us prevent things that are not the will of God.

Synonyms for *prevent* include obstruct, hinder, hamper, block, impede, interrupt, interfere, stop, put a stop to, halt, check, arrest, abort, frustrate, thwart, foil, restrain, hold back, oppose, prohibit, neutralize, and turn aside. These words help us better understand and visualize how a watchman watches.

There are three Hebrew words for *watching* or *watchman: tsaphah, shamar,* and *natsar. Tsaphah* means to lean forward, to peer into the distance, to observe, to await, to behold, to espy, to wait for, to keep the watch. *Shamar,* which we have already discussed at length, means to hedge about (as with thorns), to guard, to protect, to attend to, to be circumspect, to take heed of, to look narrowly, to observe, to preserve, to regard, to reserve or save, to lie in wait, to be a watchman. *Natsar* means to guard (in a good sense or a bad one), to conceal, to besiege, to keep, to observe, to preserve, to be a watcher. Each of these words provides insight into the function of the watchman. As the watchman peers into the distance, receiving forewarning from God, he speaks forth the word that can bring preservation, change, protection, and effective strategy.

Prophets are spiritual wardens.

As a watchman myself, I have often seen the enemy's strategies and, at times, received specific insight. I could *see* very clearly what the enemy looked like in ways ranging from the exact name of an evil spirit to specific strategic responses in spiritual warfare methods that we were to use in battle. I have also had a watchman's eye to see and understand the times and seasons of God, which influence the nature of our responses. I have watched and warned when the enemy was on the move, when we as a ministry may have been out of God's spiritual position, or when it was right to rise up and lay hold of a new season of release and blessing lest we miss what God was doing in our midst.

MAKE THE WATCH STRONG

When Nehemiah came to help the Israelites who were returning to rebuild Jerusalem, adversaries also came to oppose him. What did Nehemiah do? He set up a watch against them:

> And conspired all them together to come and to fight against Jerusalem, and to hinder it. Nevertheless we made our prayer unto our God, and set a watch against them day and night, because of them.
> —NEHEMIAH 4:8–9

Nehemiah is a picture of the apostolic ministry because apostles are builders. Whenever God is building or rebuilding something, opposition to the building process is to be expected. The only way to overcome the opposition is to set a watch against them, and that watch needs to be diligent day and night. Apostles need prophets who will assist them in building by watching and praying, seeing and announcing what they see. Apostles and prophets should work together in the building of the church.

> Also I set watchmen over you, saying, Hearken to the sound of the trumpet.
> —JEREMIAH 6:17

Because the watchmen of the Old Testament blew a trumpet to warn of coming danger, the trumpet has become symbolic of the voice of the prophet. The shamar watchmen that the Lord sets over His people have the authority to sound the trumpet. With the warning sound of the trumpet (the prophet's voice), the people will rally. The enemy's plans can be thwarted when the people respond to the sound of the trumpet. To ignore the trumpet is to invite danger.

> Make the watch strong, set up the watchmen.
> —JEREMIAH 51:12

We need to set the watchmen (the prophets) in place. No city in ancient times could be defended without a strong watch. In the same way, no church can be defended without a strong watch.

All believers are commanded to watch:

> All the people shall keep the watch of the LORD.
> —2 CHRONICLES 23:6

All believers, however, are not called to be watchmen. Watchmen are the prophetic intercessors who have a special grace to shamar the church, to keep it safe. Watchmen have the grace and discernment to see clearly the approach of the enemy, to sound the trumpet, and to rally the rest of the people to battle in prayer and action.

The word of the Lord can stir us to intercession:

> But if they be prophets, and if the word of the LORD be with them, let them now make intercession to the LORD of hosts.
> —JEREMIAH 27:18

The false prophets of Israel had no burden for intercession. They were not concerned about protecting the people. They were blind to the danger approaching. They were not fulfilling a shamar function.

Prophets help us prevent things that are not the will of God.

The prophet's primary charge, if you recall, is to stand in the gap and make up the hedge for God's people on Earth. This responsibility is where many of Israel's prophets failed:

> And the word of the LORD came unto me, saying, Son of man, prophesy against the prophets of Israel that prophesy, and say thou unto them that prophesy out of their own hearts, Hear ye the word of the LORD; thus saith the Lord GOD; Woe unto the foolish prophets, that follow their own spirit, and have seen nothing!
>
> O Israel, thy prophets are like the foxes in the deserts. Ye have not gone up into the gaps, neither made up the hedge for the house of Israel to stand in the battle in the day of the LORD.
>
> They have seen vanity and lying divination, saying, The LORD saith: and the LORD hath not sent them: and they have made others to hope that they would confirm the word. Have ye not seen a vain vision, and have ye not spoken a lying divination, whereas ye say, The LORD saith it; albeit I have not spoken?
>
> Therefore thus saith the Lord GOD; Because ye have spoken vanity, and seen lies, therefore, behold, I am against you, saith the Lord GOD. And mine hand shall be upon the prophets that see vanity, and that divine lies:

they shall not be in the assembly of my people, neither shall they be written in the writing of the house of Israel, neither shall they enter into the land of Israel; and ye shall know that I am the Lord GOD. Because, even because they have seduced my people, saying, Peace; and there was no peace; and one built up a wall, and, lo, others daubed it with untempered morter.

—EZEKIEL 13:1–10

Ezekiel was told to lay siege against the city of Jerusalem by means of a prophetic act:

Thou also, son of man, take thee a tile, and lay it before thee, and pourtray upon it the city, even Jerusalem:

And lay siege against it, and build a fort against it, and cast a mount against it; set the camp also against it, and set battering rams against it round about.

—EZEKIEL 4:1–2

This prophetic act demonstrated and released the siege of the Babylonians upon Jerusalem. It is not too much to say that this is a picture of the warfare aspect of any prophet's ministry.

Prophets have the ability to attack strongholds and to war against the powers of hell. They lay siege. They build forts against the enemy. They cast mounts and set a camp and set battering rams against the strongholds of the enemy.

Without prophets in the gates, the church cannot be victorious.

They also discover strategies that God wants them to employ against powerful enemies. It is a type of siege warfare.

Elisha instructed the king to dig the valley full of ditches:

> And he said, Thus saith the LORD, Make this valley full of
> ditches.
>
> —2 KINGS 3:16

The Moabites saw the ditches filled with water and thought they
were full of blood. The enemy was confused and thought the Israelites had smitten each other, so they felt emboldened to come right
in to the camp of Israel—where they were smitten themselves and
defeated.

Elisha gave the king a prophetic strategy to defeat the enemy.
In the same way, prophets give strategies to the church so that the
people of God can overcome the attacks of the enemy.

Prophets are a vital part of spiritual warfare. Without prophets in
the gates, the church cannot be victorious.

chapter seven

PERSONAL PROPHECY IN THE LOCAL CHURCH

G OD HAS AN unlimited number of thoughts concerning you. He also has an unlimited number of words for you. These words are more than can be numbered:

> Many, O LORD my God, are thy wonderful works which thou hast done, and thy thoughts which are to us-ward: they cannot be reckoned up in order unto thee: if I would declare and speak of them, they are more than can be numbered.
>
> —PSALM 40:5

The Bible (logos) expresses the general will of God for every believer, but a personal prophecy is more specific to the needs of individuals.

I have received hundreds of prophetic words in my lifetime. These words have brought greater clarity to my life concerning my destiny. These words have encouraged me in times of discouragement. These words have imparted strength and gifts to my life. I highly value personal prophecy, and I desire that every believer benefit from receiving the word of the Lord.

God is a personal God, and every person has a destiny in His plan. He wants each of us to choose to hear from Him. In our church, we have developed prophetic teams in order to meet the needs of many believers who desire to receive words of personal prophecy. In particular, every new member and new believer has the opportunity to receive personal prophecy. Many individuals request personal prophecy, so we have built our church to meet this need. Is it right to seek personal prophetic words, or should a person wait until such words are given only by the unction of the Holy Spirit?

I have prophesied over thousands of people with no initial unction simply because they requested ministry. I have found that as I begin to speak in faith, the unction will increase. In fact, some of the strongest prophecies I have ever received have come in spite of the fact that I had no initial unction.

The Bible expresses the general will of God for every believer, but a personal prophecy is more specific to the needs of individuals.

Prophecy can be stirred up through faith. Sometimes there is an unction to prophesy that needs no stirring, but you should know that it can be stirred up if necessary. All of the gifts can be stirred up. Teaching and preaching can be stirred up. Tongues can be stirred up. Prophecy can also be stirred up through faith and an act of the will. If you ask, you will receive:

Ask, and it shall be given you; seek, and ye shall find; knock, and it shall be opened unto you:

For every one that asketh receiveth; and he that seeketh findeth; and to him that knocketh it shall be opened.

Or what man is there of you, whom if his son ask bread, will he give him a stone?

Or if he ask a fish, will he give him a serpent?

If ye then, being evil, know how to give good gifts unto your children, how much more shall your Father which is in heaven give good things to them that ask him?

—MATTHEW 7:7–11

SEEKING A RHEMA

I am trying to challenge misconceptions about what it means to flow in the supernatural. In particular, there are several "sacred cows" that I am destroying, including this one: "Never seek a rhema." (A *rhema* is personal prophetic word from the Lord that is not something you simply read from the Word of the Lord in the Bible.) There are plenty of church leaders who do not want you ever to try to receive a word from a person with a prophetic anointing. Ministers have warned against this in their teaching because they have seen abuses. Too much deception and error have occurred in the name of "personal prophecy."

As a result, some ministers teach their people that all they need is the Bible, the Word (logos) of God. They teach their people, "If you just study the Word, you will get all of the answers that you need. Christians should never go to a service expecting someone to give them a word [rhema] from God." Consequently, many people go for years without ever getting a word from God because they have been taught to be suspicious of the supernatural flow of personal prophecy.

I understand the reasons for warning people in this way, and I know the dangers of being deceived. However, the Lord has shown me some things concerning the prophetic anointing, and I believe that it is a mistake to "throw the baby out with the bathwater." For starters, we can see in the Old Testament that people went to the prophets of God often to get the word of the Lord. They did not yet have the unction of the Holy Ghost in their own lives as we do under the new covenant, so they sought out the prophets who did have the unction. Now, even though God can speak to you individually, there are still times when you need to hear from God through the avenue of prophecy. You need to hear God's word for your life through another saint. When you receive such a word, you will know for yourself how prophecy operates, and you will be able to judge the word of the Lord by the Spirit of truth.

WHAT IS GOD'S WILL FOR YOUR LIFE?

In my years of service as a pastor, many people have come to me with questions concerning knowing the will of God for their lives. You may have questions about this as well.

You may ask, "Well, pastor, how do I really know whether this is my will or God's will?" What I always tell people is that the will of God is following the desires of your heart.

You may respond to that by saying, "Well, pastor, how do I know whether it is my desire or God's desire? How can I tell the difference between the desires I have and those that God gives me?" My answer to that is, "If your heart is pure and you really desire to do the will of God, you don't have to worry about your desires being wrong":

> Unto the pure all things are pure: but unto them that are defiled and unbelieving is nothing pure; but even their mind and conscience is defiled.
>
> —TITUS 1:15

The only time you have to be concerned about your desires being wrong is when you are in rebellion, disobedience, lust, or some other type of sin. Then you have to be careful that you don't confuse your desires with God's desires. People in a sinful spiritual state will twist or pervert God's desires. But as long as you are pure, sincere, and open before God, you can trust your desires because your heart is open to receive the desires of God rather than your own.

You will see that if you are in ministry, one of the primary ways God will lead you is by the desires of your heart. For example, if you are supposed to have a teaching ministry, God will give you the desire to teach. You will have a burning desire to teach. Jeremiah had a prophetic ministry. He was called to give the word of the Lord, and when he tried to suppress it, the desire to prophesy became like fire shut up in his bones.

You need to judge your own heart. If it is found to be pure and you are sincere, then follow the desires of your heart because God will lead you by dropping things into your spirit (that is, your heart). I believe it is the same for getting a rhema word from God.

As long as your heart is right and your motives are pure, you don't need to fear deception. God will always answer those who are pure in heart. The Bible says, "Blessed are the pure in heart: for they shall see God" (Matt. 5:8). God will give you revelation, and He will show you things to come.

According to your faith

To my surprise in one service, nearly every person in the building received a prophetic word from the Lord, even though there did not seem to be any real supernatural unction to prophesy. What happened is that I simply stirred up the gift of God that is in me. Now I know that I can lay hands upon people and prophesy to them in faith. Now I know how that gift operates, and I can flow in it.

Since every person in that building needed to hear from God, I had the ability to stir up the gift of God and to prophesy out of my gift to each one of them.

A few years ago I probably would have discouraged that type of prophesying. I very likely would have said, "If there is no supernatural unction to prophesy, if the Spirit of God doesn't really just come upon me, then I am not going to try to prophesy to everyone in the building." I also would have said, "These people should not be coming to church expecting to hear a word from God."

---

*Before there can be a counterfeit of something,
there must first be a genuine thing.*

I have since found that you should always expect to hear from God, especially in church. Too often it is religious tradition that keeps us away from receiving God's best.

> Having then gifts differing according to the grace that is given to us, whether prophecy, let us prophesy according to the proportion of faith.
>
> —ROMANS 12:6

Itching ears

> For the time will come when they will not endure sound doctrine; but after their own lusts shall they heap to themselves teachers, having itching ears.
>
> —2 TIMOTHY 4:3

I understand the principle of people having "itching ears." I know there are some people who are always trying to "get a word" from God when they go to a church service. That is why I teach that getting a word from God does not excuse you from praying and seeking Him for yourself. Prophecy is not for lazy people who do not want to pray and seek God, who would rather have someone prophesy to them. I am not referring to that type of individual. I am talking about people who are genuinely and sincerely seeking God.

There are people of God who have always asked this primary question: "Is there a word from the Lord on this situation?" They think, "We don't want to make decisions on our own. We do not want to operate out of our own minds. We want to hear from God because we know if we get the mind of God on the matter, whatever we do is going to be the right thing."

I want to urge you not to have any hesitancy in the area of receiving personal prophetic words just because so many people have fallen into deception. You cannot allow people who have dealt unwisely with a truth to keep you from walking in the truth of a word from the Lord. Every time there is a move of God, someone goes astray. But don't let that cause you to miss what God has stored up for you.

False prophets

I know there are false prophets. However, let us not forget that before there can be a counterfeit of something, there must first be a genuine thing.

There are some people who want to prophesy to you for the sake of monetary reward. They have a prophetic gift, but their purpose in prophesying is to take advantage of God's people financially. They can even be accurate in the spirit because they are prophesying out of a genuine gift. But their characters are flawed to the point that they will take advantage of God's people. Fears and financial pressures can drive people to resort to these tactics.

Ask God to keep you pure of heart and able to discern a false prophet. You will often know them by their fruits (Matt. 7:16, 20; Luke 6:44). Do not let the existence of counterfeit prophecy deter you from receiving the real thing. That would be like deciding not to pay for purchases with dollar bills because you have heard that people manufacture counterfeit ones.

Open to receive

There have been many times when I went to a meeting confused about the specifics concerning the will of God for my life. I just did not know how to accomplish what I felt He was telling me to do. I needed to hear God speak to my situation. But because the sermon was "general" in nature, an all-purpose good message, I would leave in the same state in which I came, and I would not have an opportunity to receive prophetic ministry, which is what I needed most.

It wasn't until I started seeking a rhema word from God that I got the direction I needed for my life. You will also get the direction that you need for your life if you open up your heart to the word of the Lord through personal prophecy and go to local assemblies where the believers flow accurately in the prophetic gift. Thank God for the gift of prophecy.

chapter eight

CORPORATE PROPHECY
IN THE LOCAL CHURCH

ORPORATE PROPHECY IS important to build strong local
assemblies. God edifies, exhorts, and comforts local churches
through corporate prophecy. Paul wrote to the assembly at
Corinth to give them proper instruction concerning prophecy:

> He that speaketh in an unknown tongue edifieth himself;
> but he that prophesieth edifieth the church. I would that
> ye all spake with tongues, but rather that ye prophesied:
> for greater is he that prophesieth than he that speaketh
> with tongues, except he interpret, that the church may
> receive edifying.
> —1 CORINTHIANS 14:4–5

Paul was writing because as an apostle, he had a concern for the
well-being of the local church. He desired to see the church built up
and edified in every way, and that would include through prophecy.

Although today there seems to be much emphasis on personal

prophecy, it is important for local churches to allow prophets to speak to the entire congregation as well. This is one of the ways God desires to bless and build up the local body of Christ. Churches that allow the voice of the Lord to be heard will be blessed.

It is important to give proper instruction to the local body of believers so that prophets will be able to flow in prophecy in an orderly manner. Otherwise, confusion will result.

Perhaps the biggest misconception people have about the prophetic ministry is that prophecy should be ministered in a judgmental or condemning tone of voice, as a rebuke. While some prophecies may in fact speak of judgment, this tone should be reserved for the mature prophets who function in the office of the prophet and for those who are recognized elders in the assembly. There are times when God wants to bring a word of correction to an assembly, but the majority of prophecies given to the corporate body should be given for edification, exhortation, and comfort.

DECENTLY AND IN ORDER

In the apostle Paul's first letter to the church in the city of Corinth, he gave them advice about how corporate prophecy should be delivered:

> Let the prophets speak two or three, and let the other judge. If any thing be revealed to another that sitteth by, let the first hold his peace. For ye may all prophesy one by one, that all may learn, and all may be comforted. And the spirits of the prophets are subject to the prophets. For God is not the author of confusion, but of peace, as in all churches of the saints....
>
> If any man think himself to be a prophet, or spiritual, let him acknowledge that the things that I write unto you are the commandments of the Lord....

> Wherefore, brethren, covet to prophesy, and forbid not
> to speak with tongues. Let all things be done decently and
> in order.
> —1 Corinthians 14:29–33, 37, 39–40

Paul's basic assumption was that corporate prophecy would happen on a regular basis. Therefore, it needed to be regulated so that it would contribute to edification rather than to confusion.

The early church did not have microphones or sound systems, and it appears that at times too many prophets, caught up in the spirit of prophecy, were interrupting each other in an effort to be heard. In our day and age, with the large size of many of our churches as well as the concern for maturity in those who utter prophetic words in front of the entire assembly, it is necessary to add some more advice.

For example, someone who wants to prophesy might be required to come to one of the leaders to request a microphone. What other considerations should be addressed?

Music, worship, and prophecy

As we gather together in worship, we should expect to hear the word of the Lord. Prophecy can be spoken—or it can be sung:

> What is it then? I will pray with the spirit, and I will pray
> with the understanding also: I will sing with the spirit,
> and I will sing with the understanding also.
> —1 Corinthians 14:15

As I mentioned earlier in the book, the primary Hebrew word for *prophecy* is *naba*, meaning to prophesy, to speak or sing by inspiration, to boil up, to gush forth, and to praise God while under divine influence.

Worship can cause the spirit of prophecy to be released (Rev. 19:10). As worship arises, you will see new songs and prophetic words begin to "gush forth" as the spirit of prophecy becomes strong in the assembly.

Besides being important to initiate a strong prophetic flow, music is very important to maintain it. Musicians help set the tone and atmosphere for worship. In addition, musicians can prophesy with their instruments. All of the musicians in the tabernacle of David were prophetic:

> Moreover David and the captains of the host separated to the service of the sons of Asaph, and of Heman, and of Jeduthun, who should prophesy with harps, with psalteries, and with cymbals: and the number of the workmen according to their service was:
>
> Of the sons of Asaph; Zaccur, and Joseph, and Nethaniah, and Asarelah, the sons of Asaph under the hands of Asaph, which prophesied according to the order of the king.
>
> Of Jeduthun: the sons of Jeduthun; Gedaliah, and Zeri, and Jeshaiah, Hashabiah, and Mattithiah, six, under the hands of their father Jeduthun, who prophesied with a harp, to give thanks and to praise the LORD.
>
> Of Heman: the sons of Heman: Bukkiah, Mattaniah, Uzziel, Shebuel, and Jerimoth, Hananiah, Hanani, Eliathah, Giddalti, and Romamti-ezer, Joshbekashah, Mallothi, Hothir, and Mahazioth:
>
> All these were the sons of Heman the king's seer in the words of God, to lift up the horn.
>
> —1 CHRONICLES 25:1–5

Submissive and teachable in spirit

As they minister spiritual gifts, it is extremely important for all of the saints in the local assembly to truly maintain a submissive and teachable spirit toward their pastor and their local leadership. The pastors and other leaders have been given the responsibility to be shepherds for both the people in the body and for those who are ministering in their gifts.

Input and correction given by those in authority should be eagerly received by saints, who should desire to manifest their ministry in a way that will compliment the philosophy of the local church. No prophetic team member should ever assume that he or she does not need to receive direction or correction from the pastor. (See Proverbs 12:15.)

We are all humans who are fallible and subject to error, so at some point in time while ministering, every one of us will make mistakes. Sometimes we will be aware that we have erred, but not always. Therefore, it is important to decide beforehand to be open and willing to be corrected by those over us. It is equally important for those who have been set over the congregation to exercise their authority, not to shrink back from issuing rebukes if necessary.

Those who prophesy should endeavor to present any revelation as clearly and concisely as possible.

When you make a mistake in the content or delivery of a public prophetic word, it is at these times in particular that your pastor can save your life. Remember that you are a member of a prophetic team, not a lone ranger, and that each one of us is only going to receive a partial revelation. At the same time, your pastor is responsible for the overall vision and the many functions of the local church.

Just because someone has a gift of prophecy, or even holds the office of the prophet in the local church, that never means that the person can supersede his or her local pastor.

Do not go too long

A common complaint among pastors is that many people go too long when they prophesy or minister spiritual gifts in the church. Prophets deliver elaborate words—as long as whole sermons at times.

While it is true that prophesying is like preaching in the sense that both have truth to present, it is equally true that a complicated or too-lengthy presentation can be dull or can deaden the effect of that truth.

Most congregational prophecies can be given in one minute or less—two minutes at the most. Anything longer will become extremely wearisome for others, and it will be problematic for the pastor, who is responsible for the order, schedule, and flow of the service. Those who prophesy should endeavor to present any revelation as clearly and concisely as possible.

Remember that you are a member of a prophetic team, not a lone ranger, and that each one of us is only going to receive a partial revelation.

Along the same line, a person should not feel that he or she should prophesy at every single service, since this may limit others from ministering their gifts and may even give the impression that this particular individual is trying to monopolize the prophetic or spiritual ministry of the church. Neither long-windedness nor frequency of prophesying should indicate higher giftedness in or honor for the speaker.

Flow with the order of the service

It should be obvious that prophecy is not appropriate during any part of the service when attention needs to be focused on something, in particular during the preaching, the announcements, or the altar call, when a prophetic word would be seen as an interruption. Normally, the time to flow in the gifts of the Spirit is during the worship part of the service. During the brief lull between choruses, prophets can be ready to speak. The leaders should expect and encourage manifestations of the Spirit through prophecy at this time.

When saints minister during the right time of the service, their ministry should complement the flow of the service and not contradict and change the order of the service.

For example, if the congregation is involved in exuberant and demonstrative high praises of God, it would be inappropriate to share a word about being quiet and silent before the Lord.

We believe that while God might share a key word with an individual saint that would change the order of the service, that responsibility would normally be given to the pastor and those appointed in leadership and therefore should be directed through them.

If a pastor is readily accessible during the worship service, you may share your revelation privately and allow that pastor to determine if the timing is right to share it. If not, do not be offended! You will have given what you feel God has shared with you, and it now will be in the hands of those God has appointed over the service.

A Pʀᴏᴘʜᴇᴄʏ ᴛᴏ ᴛʜᴇ Cʜᴜʀᴄʜ

The following examples of corporate prophecies released over our local assembly are edifying, exhortational, and comforting:

> The Spirit of God would have me to say that the signs and wonders recorded in the Bible are real. They happened. They are not fairy tales. The power of God is real. The miracles of God are real. The anointing of God is real.
>
> Behold, as it has been prophesied in times past, changes are coming. The spiritual climate is changing. Prophecies are going forth and changing the atmosphere. The Word of God that is going forth prophetically in this hour is changing the seasons. You will see a new move of the Spirit of God in the land. You will see God working with His mighty hand. You will see healings and miracles take place. You will see people coming, saying, "Oh, this is new."
>
> But I want you to know, My people, that in this day and hour, you must rise up in Holy Ghost power. You must not draw back. You must not be afraid to go forth. Know this, My people, that the time is ripe and the season is now for the miracles of God to come forth.
>
> Out of your belly the rivers of living waters will flow. Yes, they will flow, and they will flow, and they will flow. And then people will begin to know the power of God, and they will begin to know the miracles of God.
>
> Yes, I prophesy the signs and wonders into the church. I prophesy the miracles of God into the church and into our cities. Yes, I proclaim that people will see the glory of God. They will believe, and many will come from the north, and from the south, and from the east, and from the west.

They will come, and they will enter into a new phase of ministry and praise and glorifying the name of God. Yes, they will come because you will rise up, just as Moses did with his rod. You will speak forth into the earth. You will call down the fire of God. You will call forth the miracles of God with the authority I have given you.

Yes, the name of Jesus and the power of the Holy Ghost is in you, and you can use the rod and the authority to begin to command the signs and the wonders to come. Even as Moses did when he went into Egypt. He was afraid, but I told him, "I will be with you." I gave him signs and wonders.

Yes, God is going to even give the church signs and wonders. As you receive the signs and wonders in your own lives, you will believe just as Moses did. You will go into Egypt. And you will use the rod and the authority I have given you to proclaim the miracles of God, bring My people out of bondage, and see them set free from the pharaoh, from the taskmaster, from slavery, from cruelty, and from bondage.

Yes, many will come out of churches where they are bound and pharaohs have ruled them. Pharaohs have controlled them. Pharaohs have made slaves of many of My people. Yes, they will come out, but they won't come out until the miracles and the signs and wonders come. Yes, the miracles and the signs and the wonders will open the way for them to come out. They will come out with a mighty hand. They will come out with rejoicing. They will come out of Egypt and out of bondage. They will come through the Red Sea. Yes, they will receive the glory and the power, and the cloud and the fire.

They will go on to Canaan land, and they will go in. They will challenge the giants, they will pull down the strongholds, and they will possess their possessions, says the Spirit of God.

There is nothing—no man, no devil—that can keep My people bound. For whom the Son sets free is free indeed!

As I said in My Word, I have given you the authority and the liberty in the Spirit to be free and to be not again entangled with the yoke of bondage. But to be free that you might go into the land, challenge the giants, pull down the strongholds, receive your inheritance, walk in the blessings, and get into the land flowing with milk and honey. Yes, a land of prosperity and a land that is blessed and fruitful. Yes, it's coming, says the Spirit of God, but the signs and the wonders must come. Yes, the prophetic flow must be strong.

As I put My prophetic anointing upon Moses and upon the elders in that day, I am putting My prophetic anointing upon the leadership of My church. There will be strong prophets of God that will come up, and there will be men who will flow strongly in the prophetic. Yes, and they will train My people how to be prophets and how to flow in the prophetic. They will release the people of God to flow in the supernatural realm. They will prophesy in their homes, and they will prophesy on their jobs, and they will prophesy in the streets, and they will prophesy in the church.

The prophetic word that goes forth out of their mouths will be like a fire. It will be like a hammer that breaks the rocks in pieces. Yes, the principalities and powers, they will bow. And they will know that you are the people of God with a prophetic flow. They will come down from the high places in the land. Yes, they will see. They will see God's hand. Yes, they will tremble, and they will shake at the power of God.

When you go forth and you speak the word of the Lord, they will obey. And they will come down because the Word is like a sword. So look up, My people, and know that I am in your midst. I am there to deliver you and set you free and raise you up and thrust you into a new realm.

You will know that it is the hand of God. It is the hand of God. It is the hand of God upon the people of God in this hour to bring the people out of darkness into the marvelous light, that they might shout and dance and leap for joy. That they will know pain and sorrow no more. They will be a people prepared by the Lord to do the works of God. Then I will call them home in glory to be My bride, says the Spirit of the living God.

chapter nine

SIGNS AND WONDERS
THROUGH PROPHECY

I FIRMLY BELIEVE THAT one of the ways miracles are birthed is through prophecy. We thought that prophecy was just someone coming up and telling us some uplifting things about ourselves or prophesying some information to us about the future. Of course that is a part of the prophetic flow, but I am finding out that there is a much greater manifestation of the prophetic flow. Prophecy is much more powerful than we think.

I am finding out that the prophetic flow opens up the spirit realm for the glory of God to manifest itself in our midst.

> And it shall come to pass in the last days, saith God, I will pour out of my Spirit upon all flesh: and your sons and your daughters shall prophesy, and your young men shall see visions, and your old men shall dream dreams: and on my servants and on my handmaidens I will pour out in those days of my Spirit; and they shall prophesy: and I

will shew wonders in heaven above, and signs in the earth beneath; blood, and fire, and vapour of smoke: the sun shall be turned into darkness, and the moon into blood, before that great and notable day of the Lord come: and it shall come to pass, that whosoever shall call on the name of the Lord shall be saved.

—ACTS 2:17–21

Notice that signs and wonders follow prophecy. We prophesy, and then God begins to show signs and wonders. As soon as the people of God begin to prophesy, "Thus saith God...," things will begin to happen in the spirit realm with manifestations of signs and wonders in the natural realm. Prophecy is one of the keys to opening up the spirit realm.

Moses was a prophet of God. He had the prophetic anointing when he went into Egypt, and he performed signs and wonders. Moses is a type of the church because the church is responsible for going into Egypt (a type of the world) to deliver the people out of bondage. I believe God is going to raise up modern-day "Moseses" (modern-day prophets) who will go in with signs and wonders and cause the devil to let God's people go.

I want to see the signs and wonders. I am tired of just talking about them. I believe that one way we are going to see them is through prophetic utterances, because the prophets of God and the prophecies that they will deliver will open the way for the signs and wonders to come. I have read the second chapter of Acts many times before, but never until recently did I make the connection between prophecy and miracles.

What I am saying is that we should expect signs and wonders to follow the prophets. When the prophets prophesy into the spirit realm and the anointing of God comes upon them, they will begin to activate the miracles of God. Supernatural occurrences will begin to happen in the spirit realm through prophetic utterances.

SEEKING MIRACLES

What kinds of signs and wonders and miracles should we expect to see? I believe we should expect to see all kinds—*financial miracles, healing miracles, miracles of deliverance, supernatural signs and wonders*—in the heavens and on the earth. These things will take place, and they will confound unbelievers. The prophets of God are going to prophesy those things into manifestation. This is why it is so important to know, if we want signs and wonders in our churches, that we have to be prophetic churches.

As soon as the people of God begin to prophesy, things will begin to happen in the spirit realm with manifestations of signs and wonders in the natural realm.

There will always be some people who do not want signs and wonders. Often they are the ones who say, "Well, we don't need signs and wonders. It's OK if we get some signs and wonders and miracles, but you shouldn't chase after them."

People who say things like that have not noticed how often in the Bible a miracle was preceded by someone "chasing after" it. For example, look at the first miracle Jesus performed at the wedding in Cana.

Turning water into wine

Jesus's mother put a demand upon Him:

His mother saith unto the servants, Whatsoever he saith
unto you, do it.

—JOHN 2:5

(If there is anyone who can put a demand upon you, it is your
mother. Your mother can make you do something when no one else
can.)

And there were set there six waterpots of stone, after the
manner of the purifying of the Jews, containing two or
three firkins apiece.
Jesus saith unto them, Fill the waterpots with water.
And they filled them up to the brim.

—JOHN 2:6–7

This whole miracle is prophetic. The Lord said to fill up the water
pots with water. What does water represent in the Word of God?
It represents the Word, the cleansing of the Word. The water pots
represent earthen vessels. We are earthen vessels, and He has been
filling us with the Word.

We have more Word now than we ever had before. We have the
Word on intercession, on spiritual authority, on prophesying, on
binding and loosing in the name of Jesus, on healing, on deliverance,
on praise and worship. We have read every book. We have listened to
every tape and CD. We are full of the Word now.

And he saith unto them, Draw out now, and bear unto the
governor of the feast. And they bare it.
When the ruler of the feast had tasted the water that
was made wine…

—JOHN 2:8–9

Jesus turned that plain water into wine. This is what the Lord is doing now. What does wine represent? It represents the Holy Ghost. It is not enough to have the Word in you. You can have all kinds of scriptures in you and just be a walking Bible. The Lord wants to turn that water into wine. He wants that water to come out of you like wine, and He wants you to begin to flow in the Holy Ghost.

You can have the Word, but if you don't have the Spirit, you can't do anything with the Word. In these last days, the Lord is going to turn the water into wine. We are not going to be people of the Word only. Instead, we are going to be people of the Word and the Spirit. We are going to do miracles, prophesy, cast out devils, and flow in new songs. That's the new wine of God!

One of the problems with some Word churches is that they are still stuck on the Word. It's like they just want the water. They do not want to flow in the wine. They say, "All you need is the Word. You do not need all that Spirit stuff; just believe the Word." The Bible says the letter kills but the Spirit gives life (2 Cor. 3:6). You can have all the Word you want and still be a dead church with this type of mentality.

I agree, we do need the Word. The Word is the foundation of everything. Notice, Jesus spoke the Word before He changed the water into wine. It is risky to try to get the Spirit before you get the Word, because if you get the Spirit and you do not know any Word, you can end up getting into some strange things, thinking it is "the Spirit."

There will always be some people who do not want signs and wonders.

Many churches today have a classroom mentality. You go to church and take notes every Sunday. Well, God is more than a big classroom.

He wants to bring the church out of some of that mentality. We have sat under the teachings of someone who has bored us half to death. It is time to see some signs, wonders, miracles, the prophetic flow, and some wine. Saints are getting tired of just taking notes. They have had enough of that. They are coming out of dead churches, looking for the flow, the power, and the anointing of God.

> When he had thus spoken, he spat on the ground, and made clay of the spittle, and he anointed the eyes of the blind man with the clay, and said unto him, Go, wash in the pool of Siloam, (which is by interpretation, Sent.) He went his way therefore, and washed, and came seeing.
>
> —JOHN 9:6–7

Now, I guarantee you, Jesus didn't find that in anyone's book. You will not go into a bookstore and find this as the way to heal people's eyes. There are some things you are not going to learn from books. There are some things that are not going to line up with your theology. You have to know how to flow in the Spirit of God. You have to know how to prophesy the water into wine.

We are not going to be people of the Word only. Instead, we are going to be people of the Word and the Spirit.

Jesus's mother asked Him to do it, and even though He was reluctant to reveal His divinity too early, He did it. Then later, in the same place, Cana, we read about another "special-request" miracle:

So Jesus came again into Cana of Galilee, where he made the water wine. And there was a certain nobleman, whose son was sick at Capernaum.

When he heard that Jesus was come out of Judea into Galilee, he went unto him, and besought him that he would come down, and heal his son: for he was at the point of death.

Then said Jesus unto him, Except ye see signs and wonders, ye will not believe.

—John 4:46–48

You see, there are some people who will never believe unless they see signs and wonders. Some people are too hardheaded and blind to receive salvation. They have hard heads and hard hearts. No matter how much someone preaches to them and tells them about Jesus Christ, some people still won't believe the gospel message for themselves.

God knows some of us are too hard-hearted to just get saved, so He shows us a sign and a wonder. This is the love and mercy of the Lord drawing us into salvation.

It will take signs and wonders to convince those people that God is real. This is one of the main reasons we need to see signs and wonders. God could just say, "Forget you; just die and go to hell." On the contrary, He sends proof—especially when someone opens the way by means of an earnest request.

Often the only way for someone to have enough faith to press in to God for a miracle is in an atmosphere of desperate, God-seeking worship, which engenders prophecy. I am thankful that we serve a loving God.

God desires to birth miracles through prophecy, but it will take the church being receptive to the prophetic. Only then will we enter into the depth God desires for His people.

No prophets, no miracles

We used to think that a prophet was someone who just walked around and knew everything about you. This is not true. I flow in the prophetic, and I barely know anything about anyone. Usually, I only receive revelation about people when I lay my hands on them. That's the way my gift works. I very seldom just look at a person and know things about them.

Even through their natural discernment, anybody can look at people and tell that they have made mistakes. You do not need a dream or a vision for that. If a man is walking down the street looking wild and crazy, talking to himself, fighting and swinging his fists in the air, you do not need an anointing from heaven to see that he has a problem.

The main purpose of prophetic ministry is not to reveal secrets. It is to prophesy with such an anointing that you blast through the heavenlies and break the powers of darkness. Prophecy opens the door for the glory of God to come. Prophecy really paves the way for the Word of God to be ministered.

Prophetic ministry also paves the way for miracles. Prophecy makes it possible for a change to come in the lives of people. The prophetic worship that goes forth in the praise service even before the speaker ministers creates a change in the spiritual atmosphere. A flow of glory begins to come. By the time the speaker gets up to minister the Word of God and build the faith of the people, the place is already so filled with the glory of God that the next step is to enter right in to miracles, signs, and wonders. You've probably seen it yourself. That's why, many times, God has to bring the prophetic flow first, before the miracles occur.

Read the Bible with this in mind. Seldom will you find miracles in the Bible where there were no prophets. Read in the Book of Judges where the angel of the Lord came to Gideon and said, "Thou mighty man of valor…" and Gideon replied, "Well, where are all the miracles?" (See Judges 6:12–13.)

If we read about miracles in the Bible and we wonder why we do not see very many of them today, we do not need to wonder any longer. It is because we don't have very many prophets flowing in the prophetic anointing and bringing in the glory of God. We do not have very many prophets prophesying miracles into manifestation.

Seldom will you find miracles in the Bible where there were no prophets.

God always tells His servants, the prophets, before He does anything (Amos 3:7). You can enter into a city that is so bound by demons and so locked up by devils, with principalities and powers so strong, that you are unable to start a move of God in that city. You need the prophets to come and prophesy the mind and will of God in that place.

Some pastors don't have any miracles in their churches, and yet they rebuke their people for attending a service that does. They tell their members, "No, don't go over there. There are a lot of false prophets in the land."

I'll tell you what, pastor; why don't you get your whole church together, go down there with them, and determine whether that person is of God or not. If he is of God, then release them to attend. If he is not, then go ahead and warn your people. If people get off track, the pastor has the right to correct them. Some people do need to be corrected, but please do not kill the hunger and the desire that people have to flow in the supernatural and the glory of God. Don't kill it. Guide them, admonish them, and encourage them to go after the glory of God, because it is by the glory of God that they will experience change.

This is the reason we encourage people to come out and witness the miracles, signs, wonders, healings, and prophetic flow of the Spirit of God. Many pastors don't like it. They say, "You are taking my members."

Well, they need to come to a place like our church because those pastors are hindering their people from flowing in the Holy Spirit. They are standing in the way of God's glory.

The Scripture says that He "manifested His glory." Miracles are a manifestation of the glory of God. It is the glory of God that changes you. Miracles will change you because they introduce you to the life-changing glory of God. The apostle Peter is an example.

The Bible says that Jesus called Peter and his brother and told them to follow Him and He would make them fishers of men (Matt. 4:19; Mark 1:17). There is another account that says that Jesus told Peter to cast his net "for a draught":

> Now when he had left speaking, he said unto Simon, Launch out into the deep, and let down your nets for a draught.
>
> And Simon answering said unto him, Master, we have toiled all the night, and have taken nothing: nevertheless at thy word I will let down the net. And when they had this done, they inclosed a great multitude of fishes: and their net brake. And they beckoned unto their partners, which were in the other ship, that they should come and help them. And they came, and filled both the ships, so that they began to sink.

When Simon Peter saw it, he fell down at Jesus' knees, saying, Depart from me; for I am a sinful man, O Lord.

For he was astonished, and all that were with him, at the draught of the fishes which they had taken: and so was also James, and John, the sons of Zebedee, which were partners with Simon. And Jesus said unto Simon, Fear not; from henceforth thou shalt catch men.

And when they had brought their ships to land, they forsook all, and followed him.

—LUKE 5:4–11

When Peter drew his net, the catch was so great, it was miraculous! Upon seeing this, Peter fell at Jesus's feet and said, "Depart from me, Lord, for I am a sinful man." That miracle broke Peter and changed his life.

The glory of God is going to be orchestrated through the prophetic flow.

One of the reasons we have a lot of weak ministries and not a lot of strong ministries being birthed into the earth is because too many of them have not been birthed through miracles.

Peter's ministry was birthed through a miracle. When that net broke, he fell at the feet of Jesus and said, "Lord, depart from me." The Lord said, "Fear not, Peter; from now on, you will catch men." In other words, "This is your ministry, Peter."

Miracles are so much more than just, "Well, we had a miracle." Miracles can change people, and miracles can birth strong ministries into the earth. How many of you reading this book would like to see strong apostles, strong prophets, strong evangelists, strong pastors, and strong teachers?

I am not talking about some little weak preacher who does not walk in any supernatural ability and says he has been called by God. I am talking about strong ministries that change churches, cities, and nations. I am not talking about someone with ordination papers. Anyone can study to be a preacher, get ordination papers, and still be weak. I am talking about anointed ministries of God.

The glory of God is going to be orchestrated through the prophetic flow. The prophetic flow is going to bring in the glory. When the glory comes, miracles are going to follow. Healings are going to follow. We are going to prophesy things that are going to be established in the spirit realm. We are going to see the miracles of God come forth. We are going to see lives changed by the supernatural power of God!

The Best Is Yet to Come

I want you to notice that the best is yet to come. The Lord has kept back the good wine until the end of the age. You talk about miracles, signs, and wonders—you haven't seen anything yet!

> When the ruler of the feast had tasted the water that was made wine, and knew not whence it was: (but the servants which drew the water knew;) the governor of the feast called the bridegroom, and saith unto him, Every man at the beginning doth set forth good wine; and when men have well drunk, then that which is worse: but thou hast kept the good wine until now.
>
> —John 2:9–10

Have you ever read the Book of Acts with a longing to be back in that time? Don't worry; right now, today, He is turning the water into wine. In fact, He has saved the best wine for last, and the glory of the latter house is going to be greater than the glory of the first

(Hag. 2:9). We are going to walk in such miracles that there will be no comparison. I would rather be in this move of God than to be in the Book of Acts, because this wine tastes better.

> This beginning of miracles did Jesus in Cana of Galilee, and manifested forth his glory; and his disciples believed on him.
>
> —JOHN 2:11

Notice that miracles are manifestations of the glory of God. You may say, "Well, Brother John, why do you need miracles?" The answer is simple: we need the glory.

The main purpose of prophetic ministry is to prophesy with such an anointing that you blast through the heavenlies and break the powers of darkness.

"Well, Brother John, why do you need the glory?" The answer is because it is only the glory that will change us into the image of Jesus Christ. Prophecy comes, miracles come, the glory comes; then comes change. We get changed into His likeness.

chapter ten

PROPHECY AND THE GLORY OF THE LORD

I T IS THE glory of God that will change you into the image of
Jesus Christ. There is no way you can come into contact with the
glory of God and not be affected with a positive change.

I am sure that most people have not yet really come into contact
with the glory of God, even though they are sitting in church week
after week, hearing the Word. How do I know? I know this because
people can regularly attend church year after year, hear the Word,
and go through all the religious motions, yet they never seem to
change into the image of Jesus Christ in the least. They stay the same
as before. They are stuck.

People can pray, read their Bibles, and still never experience the
change that God desires—until they come into contact with the glory
of God. But the glory of God has not been manifested in a lot of their
churches; they have neither the unction nor the anointing of God.

It doesn't matter how much the people may *want* to change. They need something more so they can reach the fulfillment of their desires. And that something more is the glory of God.

CHANGED INTO HIS IMAGE

Scripture says we are changed into the same image from glory to glory by the Spirit of the Lord:

> Now the Lord is that Spirit: and where the Spirit of the Lord is, there is liberty. But we all, with open face beholding as in a glass the glory of the Lord, are changed into the same image from glory to glory, even as by the Spirit of the Lord.
>
> —2 CORINTHIANS 3:17–18

We must have the glory of God in our services in order to experience change. What is the glory of God? The glory of God is the tangible, manifested presence of God. What do I mean by that?

Most people understand that God is omnipresent; people realize that God is everywhere. People therefore know that God is present whether you feel Him or not. The Bible says the eyes of the Lord are everywhere, beholding the evil and the good.

And yet, chances are you are not going to feel the presence of God in a bar. Instead, you are going to feel the presence of demons, sin, and darkness.

The glory of God is something you can feel, sense, and see. In the Old Testament, the glory of God was manifested in a pillar of cloud during the day and a pillar of fire by night. It was also manifested sometimes by smoke, although it was not literal smoke but rather the palpable strength of His presence. You can see God's glory, and you can feel it.

Now, I understand that we are not supposed to be led by our

feelings. I know that we are supposed to walk by faith. But that does not mean that it is not possible to sense God's presence.

I want you to understand this one fact: *even though you may not feel God, He is in you right now.*

Many times you can go through an entire day and not feel as if you are saved. You do not feel the anointing of God. But that does not bother you. You walk by faith, and you know that God is in you whether you feel Him or not.

Regardless of whether you feel Him right now or not, you believe that He is glorious and powerful and that He has come to dwell with His people, and that means He dwells in your own heart. So do not be surprised if the tangible presence of God—what we call "the glory" of God—makes a tangible difference in you.

When the glory of God comes, when the tangible anointing and the presence of God is in a building or in a person, a person cannot help but be changed. When this happens, you are able to sense the presence of God beyond the faith realm. The influence of God is very heavy because He is manifesting Himself. His manifest presence brings a change. People cannot come into contact with the glory and presence of God without being changed.

The problem with the church is that it has a lot of teaching, preaching, Bible studies, and singing, but it never experiences the tangible presence of God, or the anointing and glory of God, on a consistent basis. This is why some of us remain the same even though we have been studying the Bible and reading religious materials all our adult lives. Unfortunately, some of us are even getting worse instead of getting better.

Hot pursuit

We need to pursue the glory and the presence of God, even though we will always have the people who don't want you to go after anything. They are the ones who say, "Be careful, now, going after those miracles. You know there are a lot of deceiving spirits out there." "Be careful about prophesying because it might not be God." "Be careful about deliverance because those devils may jump on you."

They might as well say, "Don't go anywhere. You need to stay right here and die with us. Stay right here, and don't do anything." These people will quench your zeal. They will make you stop pursuing the life-changing glory of the living God.

Do not be surprised if the tangible presence of God—what we call "the glory" of God—makes a tangible difference in you.

. I have found that when people first get saved, they have a lot of zeal. God puts this quality in them. But after a while, people begin to quench that zeal. Religious devils always tell them to sit down and be quiet. Lying spirits will say that you are *too* zealous.

All the while, I believe it is the nature of God to be zealous.

GLORY RELEASED THROUGH PROPHECY

God has ways of reviving your zeal. He has ways of helping you to recover your eagerness for more of His glory. One of the ways God's glory is released is through prophecy.

> But if all prophesy, and there come in one that believeth not, or one unlearned, he is convinced of all, he is judged of all: and thus are the secrets of his heart made manifest; and so falling down on his face he will worship God, and report that God is in you of a truth.
> —1 CORINTHIANS 14:24–25

This passage speaks of an individual coming into contact with the glory of God through the prophetic flow. He may even be an unbeliever or a person who does not know very much about God. Notice that when he comes into contact with the glory and the presence of God: (1) he will be convicted; (2) he will be discerned; and (3) he will fall on his face and say, "Surely God is in this place."

How many times do sinners come into our services and leave unchanged? Where is this "new life" that we preach about? I know sinners who will go to church, sit through the entire sermon, shake the preacher's hand, and walk out of the church door in the same condition as they came in. They have not experienced change.

Why? Because that sinner did not come into contact with the glory of God. There was no prophesying, no manifested presence of God—nothing but religion. Religion does not change anyone. That is why we *must* have prophecy.

People will say, "We don't really need that. It is not important." They don't understand that the glory of God is going to change not only unbelievers, but believers as well. If you think you can get along by just being saved and filled with the Holy Ghost, but without the prophetic flow or miracles, you are sadly mistaken. If you think you are going to become like Jesus without the glory of God, you are walking in self-deception.

You are going to be the same person you were five years ago, with the same attitude, the same mean streak, and the same weaknesses. True, you will be saved by God's grace, but you will not be any more like Jesus than you were five years ago.

It will not matter how much people are challenged by the preacher to "make a change." All of us have been told we need to change. We have been told we need to grow up. We have been told how far off we are, and we have been told to repent. We have been told all of this, but there has been no real manifestation of God's glory. We have no power to make all those changes. All of our good intentions and resolutions cannot do it. It is impossible.

We must have the glory. Otherwise we will remain stuck for the rest of our earthly lives.

Atmospheric change

The prophetic flow is one of the avenues that releases the glory of God. When the prophets begin to prophesy, it brings the glory of God into a building. It is like walking into a home where there has been a lot of cursing, strife, arguing, and fighting prior to your arrival. You can walk into a room and sense the presence of evil spirits. You also feel the confusion in the air. Words release things.

It is the nature of God to be zealous.

The same principle works in the positive with the prophetic anointing. When the prophets begin to prophesy, "Thus saith the Lord…," it charges the atmosphere with faith and with the power, the glory, and the Spirit of God, preparing the way for miracles. It is the tangible manifestation of the glory and the anointing of God that is going to bring forth miracles. You can feel it. You know God is in the house.

In conferences hosted by our church, we have a lot of prophetic songs, prophetic singing, and new songs. We stir up the gifts of God. Why? Because when you do that, you are bringing the presence of God upon the scene in a greater degree. God is already there, but you are making the environment into one that is conducive to the miracles of God and the changing of people's lives.

So next time you hear someone say, "Well, you know, we don't need to chase after miracles. You don't need to really seek out the miracles," do not listen. It is not true. Nowhere in the Bible does Jesus ever rebuke anyone for seeking after miracles, healings, or a word from Him. Never. You will not find it anywhere.

The Lord always wants us to have hungry hearts that seek after His glory and power. What must Jesus think when He hears someone discouraging a fellow believer, telling him or her, "Oh, be careful, now. You have a little too much zeal. Sit down. Don't run after that." That just kills their hungry spirits.

That just drains the life out of the zealous believer. Those same people never encourage others to seek after the glory of God. They don't offer any good alternatives. They just discourage them, shut them down, get them full of fear, and warn them, saying, "You know, if you get out there, it might be a wrong word. You might be deceived. You might get taken advantage of."

They defeat the spiritual appetite that God has put into them. This type of mind-set hinders faith. It is no wonder we have a group of dead people sitting in the church not seeking after anything. They have always been taught that it is somehow wrong.

SPIRITUAL CLIMATES

Before God does anything supernatural on a major scale, prophetic utterances must go forth. Because some spiritual climates are not conducive to miracles, we need a prophetic culture to make changes in the spiritual atmosphere of a place.

Jesus went into His hometown and could do no mighty works there because of their unbelief. The spiritual climate of that town was not conducive to miracles:

> And he could there do no mighty work, save that he laid his hands upon a few sick folk, and healed them. And he marvelled because of their unbelief. And he went round about the villages, teaching.
>
> —MARK 6:5–6

Even though He was the Son of God with the power and anointing of God without measure, when He went to Nazareth, He could not do any mighty works. In other words, the spirit of unbelief was strong in that city. Jesus laid hands on only a few sick people and healed them, but He could not do any mighty works.

Most churches and cities have a spiritual climate that is not conducive to the miracle-working power of God. Too many spirits of religion, tradition, unbelief, doubt, sin, perversion, darkness, and other spirits are holding the people back.

God always wants to minister to people. The problem is not that He is not ready; it's the people who are not ready. To get the spiritual climate to change, something needs to break.

When God went to bring Israel out of Egypt, they were not ready to just come straight out. God had to send ten plagues for the purpose of breaking something up first:

> And Moses said, Thus saith the LORD, About midnight will I go out into the midst of Egypt: and all the firstborn in the land of Egypt shall die, from the firstborn of Pharaoh that sitteth upon his throne, even unto the firstborn of the maidservant that is behind the mill; and all the firstborn of beasts. And there shall be a great cry throughout all the land of Egypt, such as there was none like it, nor shall be like it any more.
>
> —EXODUS 11:4–6

Many times something has to be broken in the spirit realm before God can accomplish what He desires to do. You may wonder why God could not just go in and bring the children of Israel out. It is because something had to be broken in the spirit realm before God's people could come out. This is the case in many instances. Something has to be broken in the realm of the spirit before God can bring people out of a particular area of bondage into a new area of liberty.

Some people never come out of certain areas of bondage because something has not been broken in the spirit realm and dealt with by the power of God. Until the power of God breaks that thing in the spirit realm, those people will remain in bondage.

Let my people go

Satan is never going to let the people go willingly. It is not his nature to do so. Satan is never going to allow a person to just go free. He will hold them. We see this when every time Moses would go to Pharaoh and say, "Let my people go," Pharaoh would harden his heart. He had to be forced to let the people go. Something has to be broken before he would let them go.

Nowhere in the Bible does Jesus ever rebuke anyone for seeking after miracles, healings, or a word from Him.

There are many people bound by religion and tradition. Those spirits are not going to let them go just because they ask them to, no matter how much of a man or woman of God they are. If I were to say, "OK, devils, just let the people go, would you, please? We want to go and serve God. We are tired of being in bondage," I do not think the devil would say, "OK, you can have them, Eckhardt."

No way! You have to break that stronghold in the spirit.

God sent Moses into Israel with the rod of authority of God to command the plagues, signs, and wonders in order to break that bondage in the spirit. Moses was a prophet.

In the same way in our time, God is raising up people with a prophetic anointing to break things in the spirit. Then God can move. This is why God wants to raise up strong prophetic churches. These churches will arise in the spirit and prophesy. The glory will come. The anointing will go forth and break the powers of darkness in the heavenly realm and open the way for signs, wonders, and deliverance.

The adversary

Because of this history, the devil has always hated the prophetic anointing, and he has always sought to kill the prophets of God.

> Therefore also said the wisdom of God, I will send them prophets and apostles, and some of them they shall slay and persecute: that the blood of all the prophets, which was shed from the foundation of the world, may be required of this generation; from the blood of Abel unto the blood of Zacharias, which perished between the altar and the temple; verily I say unto you, It shall be required of this generation.
>
> —LUKE 11:49–51

Jesus said that from the prophet Abel to Zacharias, they have been killed. Did you know Abel was the first prophet of God? The devil hates and fears the prophetic anointing, which is why he caused Cain to rise up and kill his brother. He had Jezebel try to kill all of the prophets in the land. Obadiah took more than one hundred prophets and hid them in a cave because Jezebel had cut off the prophets of God. Herodias, who was possessed by a Jezebel spirit, had John the Baptist's head cut off.

There is just something about the prophetic spirit that the devil hates because it does so much damage to his kingdom of darkness. He wants to kill the prophets and shut them up because the words that come out of their mouths are so powerful. They are like a hammer! They are so anointed that they break things in the spirit realm.

We need a prophetic culture to make changes in the spiritual atmosphere of a place.

The reason the devil tried to kill Moses when he was just a child is obvious. The devil has always tried to cut off the prophets of God. Likewise, the devil has tried, in the last generation, to kill babies through the spirit of abortion. He fears the prophets of God are going to come forth, so he is trying to kill them in the womb. Think about it. How many prophets of God have been killed through abortion?

I have news for the devil. Regardless of how many babies he kills, God will always have an ark. He put Moses in an ark when his mother put him in the little basket in the bulrushes. There are prophets who are going to be born that the devil can't kill no matter what he tries to do. He may kill some of them, but he can't kill all of them. The ones he misses are going to be the ones who tear his kingdom apart.

The devil is worried because he has missed a whole lot of them. He fears the prophetic anointing because it breaks things in the spirit. It changes the spiritual climate and tears down his kingdom.

God is raising up prophetic churches in every city. They are going to break the powers of darkness in their cities. This doesn't mean that everyone in the city is going to be saved or join your church. It does mean that God is going to deal with the powers of darkness over your cities. Their prophetic anointing is not only going to bless the people in the church building, but it will also reach into the heavenlies and break bondages. Devils and demons will have their power broken through the prophetic anointing that is upon those churches.

God wants to raise up strong prophetic churches.

Certain key churches in every city will flow in the prophetic anointing. Not every church is going to do it, but there will be certain key churches that God will raise up and put the prophetic anointing upon. The people in those churches are going to flow powerfully in prophecy, and the anointing is going to be very strong. Along with the prophetic flow, God's glory will come.

Many preachers have gone into cities that have not been broken open through the prophetic flow. They try to build a church and they struggle for years, wondering why they cannot get a ministry off the ground. It's because they have not followed through with zeal. They have not followed through with their original impetus. They need people who walk in prophetic and apostolic anointing to prophesy under the supernatural power of God. This will cause breakthroughs in the realms of darkness, pulling down the principalities and powers. It will also open the atmosphere for the glory of God and miracles to come into that city.

We need the glory. We need the prophetic flow. We need to be a prophetic people!

chapter eleven

PROPHECY WITH THE LAYING ON OF HANDS

PROPHECY WITH THE laying on of hands is a powerful way to release people into their calling and destiny. Paul told the young man Timothy, "Neglect not the gift that is in thee, which was given thee by prophecy, with the laying on of the hands of the presbytery" (1 Tim. 4:14).

A study of the power of prayer with the laying on of hands throughout the Bible is beneficial in understanding its part when combined with prophecy. Many different blessings can be imparted through the laying on of hands combined with prophecy:

> And the LORD said unto Moses, Take thee Joshua the son of Nun, a man in whom is the spirit, and lay thine hand upon him;
>
> And set him before Eleazar the priest, and before all the congregation; and give him a charge in their sight.

> And thou shalt put some of thine honour upon him,
> that all the congregation of the children of Israel may be
> obedient.
>
> —NUMBERS 27:18–20

There are some anointings received directly from the Lord, but there are others that will come exclusively through prayer with the laying on of hands.

PROMOTION AND EXALTATION

The first purpose we will discuss for the laying on of hands is promotion and exaltation. When the Lord desires to promote and exalt a person in the kingdom, He will often do it through the laying on of hands. We see this in the life of Joshua. Moses was commanded by the Lord to lay his hands upon Joshua for the purpose of establishing him as the leader for the next generation of Israel.

Every new generation needs new leadership, and the Lord promotes and exalts those with the *right* spirit. Joshua is described as "a man in whom is the spirit" (Num. 27:18). In other words, he was the one with the right spirit to be the next leader.

Joshua did not promote himself. He waited for promotion from the Lord. There are too many ministers who try to promote themselves and their ministries. They are like Adonijah, the son of David, who prepared chariots and horsemen and declared himself to be the next king (1 Kings 1). Joshua, on the other hand, was referred to as Moses's minister (Josh. 1:1). He was a faithful servant to Moses.

Because he was so faithful to Moses, the Lord promoted him to be the next leader of Israel. To do so, Moses was commanded by the Lord to lay his hands upon Joshua and transfer to him the spiritual mantle of authority for leadership.

Moses was commanded to do this openly, in front of the congregation. Everyone needed to see the person whom Moses laid his hands upon. This exemplifies the reason public ordination is so important. Moses wanted the people to be able to identify the next leader. If they watched Moses lay his hands on Joshua, there would be no doubt in their minds as to who was replacing Moses.

Many local assemblies end up in confusion after a strong leader dies, because the people don't know who is ordained by the Lord to take the reins of leadership. The church usually ends up searching for a new pastor and often votes someone into that office who is not anointed for the position. The leader did not transfer authority through the laying on of hands, and the people suffer as a result.

Moses was also commanded to give Joshua a "charge." According to the Webster definition, a *charge* is a task or responsibility given to the person who is the recipient of the laying on of hands and who now has a responsibility to fulfill. There was a charge given by Paul to Timothy (2 Tim. 4:1–2). A charge is a solemn responsibility given by the leader to the recipient.

Honor

Finally, Moses was told to put some of his "honor" upon Joshua. The word *honor* is the Hebrew word *howd*, meaning grandeur, beauty, comeliness, excellency, and majesty. Honor is a part of exaltation. When Moses laid his hands upon Joshua in the presence of the assembly, he was transferring honor to him for leadership. *Thus, the laying on of hands is a key to promotion and exaltation.*

> And Joshua the son of Nun was full of the spirit of wisdom; for Moses had laid his hands upon him: and the children of Israel hearkened unto him, and did as the Lord commanded Moses.
>
> —Deuteronomy 34:9

Leaders need honor from the Lord (and the people) in order to be effective. When you receive honor, you will be promoted and exalted into a position of leadership.

Oftentimes people fail as leaders because they have not received honor. Honor can be transferred through the laying on of hands.

Wisdom

There was also an impartation of wisdom given to Joshua through the laying on of hands. *Wisdom is also a key to promotion and exaltation.* The word *wisdom* here is from the Hebrew root *chakam*, meaning to be wise in mind, word, or act. It means to think wisely, speak wisely, and act wisely. It also means to be able to teach wisely and deal wisely. Every leader needs this chakam wisdom. Without it, you will not be capable of leading God's people.

When Moses laid his hands on him, Joshua received the honor and wisdom he needed to become the next leader of Israel. When promotion and exaltation come from the Lord, grace will also be imparted unto you to walk in a higher calling. You cannot walk in a higher calling without the ability that comes from grace. Grace was released unto Joshua through the laying on of Moses's hands.

We should promote and bless the people of God's choosing.

The hands of a spiritual leader are channels through which the power of God for promotion and exaltation flow. The honor and wisdom they walk in can be transferred to you. When you are faithful to a spiritual leader, as Joshua was to Moses, you can expect to be rewarded by the Lord with promotion. The Lord promotes those who promote His leaders.

BLESSING RELEASED

Spiritual leaders need to have a revelation of the tremendous power they can release through prophetic prayer with the laying on of hands. God will promote and bless those whom the leader lays hands upon. Leaders need to have a prophetic spirit to discern the "Joshuas" the Lord places under their authority.

I have often been checked by the Holy Ghost not to lay my hands upon some people for a release of ministry gifts and an impartation of wisdom and grace. Why? Because I discerned they did not have the right spirit. We have an unction from the Holy One and know all things (1 John 2:20). All leaders need to follow their spirits with the help of the Holy Spirit. We should promote and bless the people of God's choosing.

Remember, the Lord is always promoting people based on faithfulness and His purpose. As one generation serves the Lord and departs, another must take its place. The laying on of hands is an important guideline that will help us in this *transfer of authority*. There are vacancies in the Spirit because there is no one to fill the void.

The kingdom will suffer if there are no Joshuas to fill the void of Moses. The devil does not want to see the Joshuas promoted. He does not want to see honor and wisdom released to the next generation for promotion and exaltation. He does not want the church to understand and walk in the power that is released *through the simple act of the laying on of hands.*

However, the Lord has given the church knowledge and revelation of these things, by His Spirit, through the Word of God. We are not just laying empty hands on empty heads; we are learning how to flow with God's methods and how to release the power of God in the earth.

We are releasing the next generation of apostles, prophets, evangelists, pastors, and teachers. Once local churches receive the revelation of the power of the laying on of hands and practice this doctrine, we will see a greater manifestation of God's power through His people. We will see stronger leaders and stronger churches come forth.

The power of blessing

See what happens when a blessing is released:

> And Joseph took them both, Ephraim in his right hand toward Israel's left hand, and Manasseh in his left hand toward Israel's right hand, and brought them near unto him.
> And Israel stretched out his right hand, and laid it upon Ephraim's head, who was the younger, and his left hand upon Manasseh's head, guiding his hands wittingly; for Manasseh was the firstborn.
> —GENESIS 48:13–14

Blessing through the laying on of hands is a way to promotion and exaltation. Israel (Jacob) blessed the two sons of Joseph. To *bless* simply means to praise or speak well of. The Lord told Abram, "I will bless thee and make thy name great." (See Genesis 12:2.) *Blessing is a key to having a great name.* Israel blessed his grandsons by laying his hands upon them and speaking prophetically over their lives.

As one generation serves the Lord and departs, another must take its place.

However, through the leading of the Lord, he switched the birth order. He crisscrossed his hands to lay his right hand upon the younger son's head (Ephraim) and his left hand upon the older son's head (Manasseh). The right hand was the hand of greater blessing.

While each son received a blessing because Israel spoke well of them both, Ephraim received a *greater* blessing since Israel spoke greater things over his life. Blessing through the laying on of hands, accompanied by the prophetic word, does not depend on natural birth order. The call of God is based on *grace*. The Lord chooses whom He wills.

Scripture says Israel guided his hands "wittingly." He was led of the Lord in the way to lay his hands upon the two sons. It should be the same for us. The laying on of hands is not some arbitrary practice. It is something that should be divinely directed by the Lord. Exaltation, promotion, and the future of their descendants depended upon this blessing through the prophetic word and the laying on of hands.

> And Joseph said unto his father, Not so, my father: for this is the firstborn; put thy right hand upon his head.
>
> And his father refused, and said, I know it, my son, I know it: he also shall become a people, and he also shall be great: but truly his younger brother shall be greater than he, and his seed shall become a multitude of nations.
>
> —Genesis 48:18–19

To this extent, the greater blessing came through the right hand and the lesser blessing through the left. The power of blessing released, through the laying on of Israel's hands, would affect the future generations of the two sons of Joseph. In addition, this single act would affect entire nations of people! Your destiny and the destiny of your children can hinge on the laying on of your hands! This alone should cause us to approach this subject with reverence and awe. The laying on of hands—with prophetic revelation—is foundational to the plans and purposes of God in the earth.

Israel laid hands upon the two sons of Joseph when they were children. Jesus also laid His hands upon children (Matt. 19:13–15). There is a strong precedent in the Word for laying hands on the children to bless them. That is because there is an ability in our hands to affect entire generations to come!

TYPES OF PROMOTION

There are three types of promotion: (1) self-promotion, (2) promotion by other people, and (3) promotion by God. Self-promotion and promotion by other people can be fleshly and demonic. There is, however, a promotion by other people that can be of God. By the leading of the Lord, Moses promoted Joshua by placing honor upon him.

To *promote*, according to Webster, means to advance in station, rank, or honor; to contribute to the growth or prosperity of. To *exalt* means to raise in rank, power, or character; to elevate by praise or in estimation.

> For promotion cometh neither from the east, nor from the
> west, nor from the south. But God is the judge: he putteth
> down one, and setteth up another.
> —PSALM 75:6–7

Both promotion and exaltation come from God, but often they are transmitted through a person. When the Lord desires to promote and exalt you, He will often send a person into your life to *bless* you. I desire to associate with those who can bless me. I seek not to promote myself but to allow the Lord to lead me into divine relationships. There are people I am to meet and associate with, according to the Lord's plan for my life, chosen before the foundation of the world.

The Lord desires to place you under a mentor who can lay hands upon you and bless you. It is an important key to promotion and exaltation that come from the Lord. This is why finding the right mentor is so important. By understanding what the Bible teaches about the *laying on of hands* as it relates to *promotion and exaltation*, you will be in a position to receive the blessings the Lord has prepared for all of His children.

Humility

There is, of course, more to being honored and exalted than the laying on of hands. *Humility is also a requirement for promotion and exaltation.* The word of the Lord tells us that "before honour is humility" (Prov. 15:33), and humility comes before exaltation. "He that shall humble himself shall be exalted" (Matt. 23:12).

This is why I believe the Lord uses the laying on of hands as a way of promotion and exaltation. Although promotion and exaltation come from the Lord, they often come through human channels.

The Lord will cause us to humble ourselves and *submit* to another to receive the impartation we need. This submission will result in our mentors laying hands on us to impart spiritual blessings.

A prideful and rebellious spirit will keep you from submitting to another to receive spiritual endowments through the laying on of hands. Counter the independent, self-oriented spirits of pride and rebellion with true humility.

The Lord will not promote and exalt a person apart from humility. He will lead us into divine relationships to receive the impartation we need. Joshua submitted to Moses. Elisha submitted to Elijah. Timothy submitted to Paul. They all received impartation because of submission. I have seen ministers who were unwilling to submit to proper spiritual authority and, as a result, never received the spiritual deposits necessary to fulfill their calls.

All spiritual gifts and endowments come from heaven:

> John answered and said, A man can receive nothing,
> except it be given him from heaven.
>
> —JOHN 3:27

People cannot give you these things. They come directly from the throne of grace. People are simply *channels* through which God's grace can come.

God has set up an authority structure in the kingdom of God, and He operates through and honors this authority. The church has been given the keys of the kingdom. We have the power of binding and loosing. And since the Lord has given authority to the church, He will release His power and blessing through the church.

The Spirit of God honors the laying on of hands as a channel through which He comes.

When you submit to proper spiritual authority, God's power and blessing can be released on your behalf through the laying on of hands. When you rebel against the authority the Lord has established in the church, you will not receive all of the spiritual impartation available to you.

The Lord will use your spiritual leaders as channels to bless you. They are channels for promotion and exaltation. As you submit to your spiritual leaders, they will in turn lay hands upon you for promotion and exaltation. A leader can place some of his honor upon you, just as Moses did unto Joshua.

GIFTING AND EQUIPPING

The second purpose of the laying on of hands is for *gifting and equipping*, for the purpose of doing the works of Jesus:

> Then laid they their hands on them, and they received the Holy Ghost.
>
> —ACTS 8:17

> And when Paul had laid his hands upon them, the Holy Ghost came on them; and they spake with tongues, and prophesied.
>
> —ACTS 19:6

The first gift every believer needs is the gift of the Holy Ghost. He will empower and equip you for service. You will never be equipped to do the works of Jesus without receiving the Holy Ghost. Gifting and equipping are necessary for effective ministry. The Lord would never send us forth as ministers of the New Testament without *first* gifting and equipping us.

It would be unfair for Him to give us responsibility without also giving us *divine ability*. We must have the ability to carry out what we have been commissioned to do. Prayer with the laying on of hands is the primary way for saints to receive this gifting and equipping. By this means, the power of God is released, giving the recipient the grace needed to fulfill the call of God.

In the following verse from Scripture, notice that gifting and calling go together:

> For the gifts and calling of God are without repentance.
>
> —ROMANS 11:29

The Lord will gift you for what He has called you to do. Every believer has been called to do the works of Jesus. (See John 14:12.) This includes preaching, teaching, healing, and deliverance. All believers need the gift of the Holy Ghost to fulfill that call.

The first thing the apostles would do after people believed was lay hands upon them to receive the Holy Ghost. The Spirit of God honors the laying on of hands as a channel through which He comes. If the Holy Ghost honors the laying on of hands, how much more should we as believers honor this practice?

As the apostles would lay hands upon believers, the Holy Ghost would come upon them. We, as believers, can walk in the same *spirit of faith* as we lay hands upon believers. We can expect the Spirit of God to come upon them because He has chosen to honor the laying on of hands.

We can expect the same results because we are following biblical order established by the apostles. Prayer with the laying on of hands is a foundational doctrine we can stand on in faith to receive supernatural results. We have the Word of God backing us as we lay hands upon people to receive the Holy Ghost. In this way, we are gifting and equipping them for service.

Tremendous power is released into the earth as a result of ordinary believers walking in the fullness of power that comes through receiving the Holy Ghost:

> And Ananias went his way, and entered into the house; and putting his hands on him said, Brother Saul, the Lord, even Jesus, that appeared unto thee in the way as thou camest, hath sent me, that thou mightest receive thy sight, and be filled with the Holy Ghost.
>
> —ACTS 9:17

Here we see the Lord using a disciple named Ananias to lay hands upon Saul to receive the Holy Ghost. Saul was receiving the gifting and equipping he needed to begin his ministry. Again, we see an illustration of the principle that when the Lord desires to release His power into the earth, He often does it through the laying on of hands. By using Ananias to lay hands on Saul, the Lord released into the earth one of the strongest ministry gifts the church has ever known.

Although Paul's call and ministry were unique in that he did not receive his revelation of the gospel from man, the Lord had an ordinary disciple lay hands upon him at the start of his ministry. This was a sovereign move of God to bring both Paul and Ananias together.

Prayer with the laying on of hands is a foundational doctrine we can stand on in faith to receive supernatural results.

I believe Paul's pride received a devastating blow on the road to Damascus. He also had to submit to Ananias in the matter of the laying on of hands and receiving a word from God through a stranger. The laying on of hands can be a humbling experience on the part of the recipient.

Sometimes people will say, "I don't need anyone to lay hands upon me. I can receive all I need directly from God." While it is true that you can receive the Holy Ghost without the laying on of hands, the Lord will often have you submit to the laying on of hands in order to receive the blessing and power you will need to fulfill your destiny. Any spiritual pride that you may have will be destroyed, and you will be much more open to receiving the grace and the gifting that God wanted to give you. We should welcome the people whom God sends into our lives for the purpose of imparting blessings to us through their prayers with the laying on of hands.

chapter twelve

IMPARTATION THROUGH PROPHETIC MINISTRY

IN ORDER TO better understand God's power through the laying on of hands, we must understand the subject of impartation. The word *impart* is taken from the Greek word *metadidomi*, meaning to give over or to share. When something is imparted, it has been conveyed from one person to another.

The apostle Paul had a desire to impart unto the saints "some spiritual gift":

> For I long to see you, that I may impart unto you some spiritual gift, to the end ye may be established.
>
> —ROMANS 1:11

In the Weymouth translation of this passage, it reads, "For I am longing to see you, in order to convey to you some spiritual help, so that you may be strengthened."[1]

Therefore, what Paul was imparting was meant to be of spiritual help to the saints. Spiritual impartations are given to help us fulfill the will of God for our lives. This is a part of equipping. We become equipped to do the work of the ministry through impartation.

ESTABLISHED AND STRENGTHENED

The result of impartation is establishment. In some translations, "to the end ye may be established" is translated "to strengthen you" or "and so give you fresh strength." Thus, the believer is equipped with *fresh strength* as a result of impartation.

One important channel by which this equipping of fresh strength is imparted is through the laying on of hands. We know that Timothy received a spiritual gift through the laying on of hands by Paul. This is impartation from one ministry gift to another. Timothy was strengthened and equipped for his ministry as a result of impartation.

Impartation can also come through association. In this way, there will be a transference of anointing from or to the people you associate with. With or without an accompanying laying on of hands, we can receive through impartation from the ministries we submit to and associate with.

There are, I believe, divine relationships ordained by the Lord before the foundation of the world. There are certain people the Lord has predestined for you to link up with in the Spirit. They will have the spiritual deposits you need. You can receive an extra measure of these deposits through the laying on of hands.

It is the will of God that the church operate in all of the gifts and anointing it needs as we await the return of our Lord. It is not the will of God for us to lack any necessary gift.

Paul wrote to the local church in Corinth:

> I thank my God always on your behalf, for the grace of
> God which is given you by Jesus Christ; that in every

thing ye are enriched by him, in all utterance, and in all knowledge; even as the testimony of Christ was confirmed in you: so that ye come behind in no gift; waiting for the coming of our Lord Jesus Christ: who shall also confirm you unto the end, that ye may be blameless in the day of our Lord Jesus Christ.

—1 CORINTHIANS 1:4–8

God has given us the means to obtain all we need. He is ready and willing to gift and equip us with all the spiritual grace we need to complete our commission: *to preach the gospel to all nations and make disciples of all men* (Matt. 28:19).

If we are lacking in spiritual power, it is not the Lord's fault. He has provided everything we need, but we must take advantage of it. This is why it is so important to understand the teaching and wisdom about the laying on of hands. The laying on of hands is a primary channel through which we can receive the spiritual gifts we need as we work and wait for the coming of the Lord.

Strong, not weak

There is really no excuse for so much weakness in the body of Christ. I am so tired of weak Christians and weak churches. A weak and spiritually anemic church is the result of a lack of spiritual gifts. Far too many churches are deficient in spiritual gifts because they do not know how to release God's power through the laying on of hands. When you are deficient in spiritual gifts, you will not be the able ministers of the New Testament that the Word talks about.

God is ready and willing to gift and equip us with all the spiritual grace we need to complete our commission.

The Word tells us to be strong in the Lord and in the power of His might. We are to be strengthened with might by God's Spirit in the inner man. It takes spiritual strength to cast out devils, heal the sick, raise the dead, and reach the lost. Without the gifting and equipping that come through impartation, the church becomes traditional and ceremonial. Many have a form of godliness but deny the power thereof. The kingdom of God is not in word but in power! There is too much preaching of the letter of the law without the power and demonstration of the Holy Spirit.

If you associate with strength, you will become strong. You become like the people you associate with. Don't allow yourself to become weak by linking up with the wrong kind of believer. It is important to associate with strong ministries and receive impartation through the laying on of hands. You need to associate with strong churches and strong ministries. If you associate yourself with weakness, you will become weak.

You must find your own company and fellowship there. You must find a New Testament church that believes in and practices the doctrine of the laying on of hands. You need strong apostles and prophets to lay hands upon you and impart spiritual gifts and strength. Then you will be able to rise up and be the strong believer the Lord expects you to be.

IMPARTATION OF SPIRITUAL GIFTS

Beyond the gifting and equipping that every believer needs to do the works of Jesus, there is special gifting needed for the fivefold ministry. Not everyone is called into the ministry of apostle, prophet, evangelist, pastor, or teacher. There is gifting and equipping that will come at the time of separation for a specific ministry. This gifting and equipping can be received through prophetic presbytery:

> Neglect not the gift that is in thee, which was given thee by prophecy, with the laying on of the hands of the presbytery.
>
> —1 TIMOTHY 4:14

The *presbytery* is the group of ruling elders in a local church or a group of local churches. Elders need to flow in prophecy along with the laying on of hands. This is one of the ways Timothy received gifting and equipping for his call into the ministry. This is a biblical pattern for ordination. (See the next chapter for a much more complete discussion of the prophetic presbytery.)

At the time of ordination, those being ordained need to have prophetic utterances spoken over them, with the laying on of hands for the impartation of spiritual gifts. Each ministry has a prophetic destiny that needs to be revealed and activated through the *prophetic presbytery*. The laying on of hands imparts the spiritual gifts needed to fulfill the call. As a result, the person or group receives the word of the Lord concerning their life and ministry plus the power and ability needed to fulfill it. It happens through the laying on of hands.

When ministry gifts do not receive this kind of ministry, they often lack the prophetic direction and spiritual ability necessary to fulfill their call. The laying on of hands has become ceremonial and traditional in some churches, lacking the power it had in the early church to gift and equip ministers. The Lord desires to restore to the church the prophetic presbytery, with the laying on of hands, in its fullness. When you receive gifting and equipping, you will become able ministers of the New Testament.

Divine pattern

If we desire to have Bible results, we must begin to do things the Bible way. The early church left us a divine pattern to follow. If we follow this pattern, we will begin to see supernatural results:

> Wherefore I put thee in remembrance that thou stir up the gift of God, which is in thee by the putting on of my hands.
>
> —2 TIMOTHY 1:6

Paul is reminding Timothy to stir up the gift he received through the laying on of hands. One translation says, "…to fan the flame of that special grace." The gift of God can be referred to as special grace. This gifting and equipping go beyond the gift of the Holy Ghost, which is available to all believers and is known as "common grace." Special grace is needed to fulfill a special call into the ministry.

Paul warned Timothy not to neglect the gift but rather to stir it up. The gifts of God must be continually stirred up by faith. A person can receive gifts through the laying on of hands and not operate in them because of spiritual neglect. The recipient of special grace through the laying on of hands has a responsibility that comes with the gift. This is in line with the charge often given when hands are laid upon an individual to ordain him or her to the service that God has indicated.

The charge is a solemn responsibility the recipient must keep. Unto whom much is given, much is required (Luke 12:48). Don't be too anxious to receive impartation through the laying on of hands unless you are committed to use what you receive.

The gifts received in this way are what I call spiritual deposits. The Lord desires to make spiritual deposits in all of us. He wants us to use these deposits to be a blessing to others. In essence, the Lord expects returns on His deposits. Just as we expect interest on bank deposits, the Lord expects interest on the gifts He deposits into us.

The Lord equips us with gifts, and He expects us to do something with what He has given us. He has equipped us to do the works of Jesus. He expects apostles, prophets, evangelists, pastors, and teachers to take seriously their responsibility to perfect the saints and build up the body of Christ.

Every believer needs to ask himself or herself this question: Am I equipped to do what the Lord has called me to do? If you are not, then how can you fulfill your call?

Special grace is needed to fulfill a special call into the ministry.

Is the laying on of hands for gifting and equipping strong enough in our local assemblies? Is there enough teaching on this subject for the saints to function effectively in ministry? If not, how can we become better equipped to do what the Lord has called us to do?

Every local church should lay hands upon people to receive the Holy Ghost. Every believer needs to be baptized with the Holy Ghost. All believers need to be equipped to do the works of Jesus. Every local church should have elders who flow strongly in the laying on of hands. Without these means of equipping and strengthening, the local church cannot even accomplish the minimum of what God established it for. The saints need the spiritual strength that is released through the laying on of hands.

These things will become stronger in our assemblies if we teach and emphasize their importance. The things of God operate and are received by faith. Faith comes by hearing the Word of God. As we teach the Word of God in this area, the leadership will be able to release gifts, and the saints will be able to receive gifts through the laying on of hands.

Just as we expect interest on bank deposits, the Lord expects interest on the gifts He deposits into us.

Once this truth is taught, received, and practiced, the saints will be gifted and equipped. Gifting and equipping won't just happen, but we must teach about and practice the laying on of hands. It will change a local church. Our churches will be full of the gifts of the Spirit. We will see stronger anointings come forth in our churches.

Don't draw back from teaching and practicing the laying on of hands. Prophetic prayer with the laying on of hands is foundational for equipping the saints to perform the will of God. When you lay hands on people, do it in faith. Expect the Lord to move through the laying on of hands.

SEPARATING AND RELEASING

In the previous chapter, you learned that the first purpose for the laying on of hands is promotion and exaltation, which includes the impartation of wisdom and honor. The laying on of hands imparts blessing to the person being prayed for. The laying on of hands, together with prophetic, prayerful declarations, also releases gifts and equips people to fulfill their callings.

A third purpose for the laying on of hands is to *separate and release* ministry gifts into the earth. Barnabas and Paul were separated and

released into their apostolic ministries through the laying on of
hands:

> As they ministered to the Lord, and fasted, the Holy Ghost
> said, Separate me Barnabas and Saul for the work where-
> unto I have called them.
>
> And when they had fasted and prayed, and laid their
> hands on them, they sent them away.
>
> So they, being sent forth by the Holy Ghost...
> —Acts 13:2–4

In this case, it was accompanied by prayer and fasting. Again, we
see the principle that when the Lord desires to release His power into
the earth, He often does it through the laying on of hands.

There are several points I want to emphasize in these verses.
Number one is the Holy Ghost said that they should "separate"
Barnabas and Saul. Barnabas and Saul were now to be *separated* to
the ministry that they had been previously called to. The Holy Ghost
had already called them to be apostles, but they had not yet been
separated to that call. There is a time period between calling and
separation called *preparation*. That period of time was now finished.
The laying on of hands was for their separation to their ministry.

There is a time for calling, a time for preparation, and a time for
separation. The *calling* is sovereign, and it comes by the Holy Ghost.
The preparation for the call depends upon the individual's willing-
ness to pray, study, and develop the character of Christ. There are
different periods of preparation for different people. For some it is
longer than others. Patience is required until the time of separation
to the actual ministry. The Holy Ghost knows the time of separation.
Just because a person has a call does not mean that he or she is ready

to function in that capacity. The call is only the beginning, followed by preparation, then separation.

The gifting and equipping for ministry can also come at the time of separation for ministry. In other words, you can receive the grace you need to fulfill your call, at the time of separation, through the laying on of hands.

People often go into ministry *prematurely*, without the necessary equipping and separation that are accomplished through the laying on of hands. This is one reason why so many ministry gifts are weak and ineffective. It is not because they have not been called, but because they have not been properly equipped and separated. *Separation has to be done in proper spiritual timing.* It should not be done prematurely, but rather, it should always be done by the leading of the Holy Ghost.

Notice also that the apostles did not leave the church at Antioch without first receiving the blessing of the leaders of the church. The Holy Ghost honors submission to the presbytery that comes through the laying on of hands. After Paul and Barnabas were released to minister, they remained accountable to the leaders of the church at Antioch. They reported to this church after their missionary journeys. They were submitted and accountable to the ones who had laid hands upon them.

People often go into ministry prematurely, without the necessary equipping and separation that are accomplished through the laying on of hands.

Barnabas and Saul had to be separated from the local church to travel as apostles. They had to be released by the church. They were not *sent forth* by the Holy Ghost until they were *sent away* through laying on of hands by the presbytery. Even though the Holy Ghost is divine, He works through men. This is one of the ways the Holy Ghost separates and releases ministry gifts into the earth.

We see here the authority that is given to the local church by the Lord. The Lord honors and recognizes this authority because it comes from Him. That authority to separate and release ministry gifts is released through the laying on of hands.

Based on this biblical pattern seen in the church at Antioch, there are several questions to ask if you feel called into the ministry:

1. First, do you have the necessary preparation (training, study, wisdom, character) to be separated to the call?

2. Do you have the necessary gifting and equipping to fulfill the call? (This will often come at the time of separation.)

3. Is it the right time for separation to that call?

Remember, the calling is sovereign and comes from God through the Holy Ghost, but the preparation is dependent upon your response to the call. You have a part in the preparation by studying, praying, and developing the character of Christ, and this will take different amounts of time for different people.

The gifting, equipping, and separation can be done through laying on of hands after the calling and preparation have been established, but the separation depends on Spirit-led timing. In turn, gifting, equipping, and separation will hinge on how well developed the church is in the area of prophetic presbytery. The body of Christ as a whole needs more mature prophets so that this process can function according to the biblical pattern.

RELEASING HELPS

Deacons were released to serve through the laying on of hands by the apostles:

> ...whom they set before the apostles: and when they had prayed, they laid their hands on them.
>
> —ACTS 6:6

The result was "the word of God increased; and the number of the disciples multiplied in Jerusalem greatly" (v. 7). Deacons were set in the church, thus freeing up the apostles to give themselves to prayer and the ministry of the Word. Thus, the laying on of hands is also a channel to release the helps ministry in the church.

In this case, the Holy Ghost did not separate them; the church separated the seven men who were full of the Holy Ghost and wisdom, and the church set them before the apostles. The apostles gave their approval to the selection through the laying on of hands.

Later, the apostle Paul gave a list of qualifications for deacons. (See 1 Timothy 3:10.) He wrote that they must first be proved before the laying on of hands to set them in the church, releasing them to serve. Just as ministers need to be released to minister in their call, deacons also need to be released to serve through the laying on of hands.

As I have already indicated, the reason that many churches do not have the ability to gift, equip, and separate people properly into their callings is because they have no prophetic presbytery. The elders (presbytery) of the local church must be able to flow prophetically and be established in a foundational understanding of the laying on of hands in order to release people into every calling necessary for healthy, strong church life.

After people have been gifted, equipped, and separated through the laying on of hands, they can then be released. Prophecy, prayer, and fasting should accompany the laying on of hands to release all of the grace and power needed for effective ministry.

CHECKS AND BALANCES

Here is a piece of advice from Paul to Timothy:

> Lay hands suddenly on no man.
> —1 TIMOTHY 5:22

I believe this verse applies to specific ordination, but it is also a general principle to be followed by the church. The word *suddenly* has to do with spiritual timing. We should not proceed in haste, but rather, we should be led by the Holy Ghost as to the proper time to lay hands on people to ordain and separate them.

The Holy Ghost knows the call, character, and preparation of every believer. He knows the proper time to tell us when to lay hands upon people for equipping, gifting, and separation. Laying on hands prematurely can be harmful for the believer and also for the church. I cannot emphasize enough the importance of being sensitive to the Holy Ghost in the area of the laying on of hands.

In a general sense, this is also a warning to the church concerning the laying on of hands without using discernment first. This is especially true because of the possibility of transference of spirits. There is such a thing as a dangerous transference of spirits. Just as Joshua received a spirit of wisdom from Moses through the laying on of hands, a person can also receive the wrong spirit from a wrong-spirited minister who lays hands on him or her. Paul warned the Corinthians about receiving "another" spirit (2 Cor. 11:4). In the Old Testament, the sins of the people were symbolically transferred to the scapegoat by the laying on of hands (Lev. 16:21). The Lord does not want you to be a scapegoat for somebody else.

There are two extremes to avoid as a believer: First, being so afraid of an evil transference until you become paranoid of anyone laying hands upon you, or you laying hands upon anyone. Second, allowing everyone to lay hands upon you, or you laying your hands upon everyone. "Lay hands suddenly on no man" gives us a balance. It does not tell us not to lay hands on people, but rather, *not* to do it *too hastily.*

Just don't be too quick to lay hands on people or to allow people to lay hands on you. Allow yourself to be led by the Holy Ghost. Don't walk in fear, but walk in faith; and keep yourself covered by the blood of Jesus. The laying on of hands is a powerful thing; do not misuse it.

HEALING AND DELIVERANCE

> Now when the sun was setting, all they that had any sick with divers diseases brought them unto him; and he laid his hands on every one of them, and healed them.
>
> And devils also came out many, crying out, and saying, Thou art Christ the Son of God.
>
> —LUKE 4:40–41

The fourth purpose for the laying on of hands is for *healing and deliverance.* In the passage above, notice the response of demons to the laying on of hands. When the anointing flows through the hands into the bodies of those oppressed by the devil, it heals them. It also stirs up demons and drives them out.

God anointed Jesus of Nazareth with the Holy Ghost and power to heal those who were oppressed of the devil (Acts 10:38). Sickness is an oppression of the devil. It is no wonder that the demons reacted as Jesus ministered through the laying on of His hands. Demons hate the laying on of hands. They do not want you to lay your hands on sick people and drive them out.

Some have been taught to never lay hands on demonized people, but this is not the teaching of Jesus. He laid His hands upon people who had demons and drove them out. I am not advocating that believers look for everyone who is demonized to lay hands upon, but I am saying that you should not fear laying hands upon people to drive out demons. All deliverances do not require the laying on of hands, but it is a valid administration of the ministry of deliverance.

Virtue

If a believer is filled with the power of the Holy Ghost, he or she is filled with *virtue*. Sometimes the word *dunamis* is translated as *power*, and at other times, as *virtue*. Virtue and power (*dunamis*) are the same. When the woman with the issue of blood touched the hem of the garment of Jesus, He perceived virtue (*dunamis*) had gone out of Him. Healing virtue can flow into the bodies of the sick through the laying on of hands.

This virtue can be used to heal the sick and drive out evil spirits. Spirit-filled believers can lay hands on the sick and expect to transfer virtue into their bodies. This virtue will drive out sickness and disease, which are the works of the devil.

The disciples were told by Jesus, "Ye shall receive power [*dunamis*, virtue], after that the Holy Ghost is come upon you" (Acts 1:8). Spirit-filled believers are walking reservoirs of the healing anointing. You carry with you the virtue of Christ. The Lord desires to release His virtue into the earth through the laying on of your hands. That is how it worked for Paul, even in unusual situations:

> And it came to pass, that the father of Publius lay sick of
> a fever and of a bloody flux: to whom Paul entered in, and
> prayed, and laid his hands on him, and healed him.
>
> —ACTS 28:8

Paul started a healing meeting on the island of Malta (also called Melita) through the laying on of his hands. "So when this was done, others also, which had diseases in the island, came, and were healed" (Acts 28:9). He was illustrating the prediction in the Gospels: "They shall lay hands on the sick, and they shall recover" (Mark 16:18).

There was enough healing virtue in the hands of Paul to heal every sick person on that island. No wonder the devil hated him, and no wonder demons hate and fight the doctrine of the laying on of hands. They do not want believers to know the power and virtue that is released through the laying on of hands. They want to hide the truth from you because the laying on of hands is the *foundation* of releasing the power of God into the earth.

This is a sign that should follow every believer. Every believer should be able to lay hands on the sick and expect them to recover. This is different from the presbytery laying on hands to equip through impartation. Every believer is not a part of the presbytery. The Holy Ghost honors the laying on of hands by the presbytery when it comes to separating ministry gifts, and every believer cannot lay hands upon ministers to release them the way the presbytery can. But every believer can lay hands upon people to receive the Holy Ghost for healing and deliverance. This is an honor God has given to all His saints.

It is the responsibility of the fivefold ministry to train believers in these areas. The Lord wants to release His people in the area of the laying on of hands. All believers should be trained and released to lay hands on the people for healing, deliverance, and the baptism of the Holy Spirit.

Jesus loosed the woman from a spirit of infirmity through the laying on of hands:

> And he was teaching in one of the synagogues on the sabbath. And, behold, there was a woman which had a spirit of infirmity eighteen years, and was bowed together, and could in no wise lift up herself. And when Jesus saw her, he called her to him, and said unto her, Woman, thou art loosed from thine infirmity.
>
> And he laid his hands on her: and immediately she was made straight, and glorified God.
> —LUKE 13:10–13

There was an immediate, instantaneous healing. Thus, we have the power of loosing and the laying on of hands. Loosing people is a manifestation of deliverance. The church has been given the power of binding and loosing. One of the ways we can operate in loosing is through the laying on of hands.

In this particular case, the woman received her healing through deliverance. There are some people who will not be healed until evil spirits are cast out. There is a fine line between healing and deliverance. These two ministries often overlap. The laying on of hands is effective in both cases. Once the evil spirit is cast out, the damage done to that part of the body can then be healed. In many cases, spirits of death and destruction will also need to be cast out, along with a spirit of infirmity. Unforgiveness and bitterness also need to be renounced, in most cases, before healing and deliverance through laying on of hands can be effective.

Working in unison with the laying on of hands is a *command* to every believer. Believers need to understand the subjects of authority and power in addition to the laying on of hands.

The understanding of the power of laying on of hands when coupled with prophecy will help believers release deliverance, healing, promotion, and blessing. We often lay hands on people when we prophesy. I have seen people healed and delivered through prophecy and the laying on of hands. I have personally received tremendous impartation through prophecy with the laying on of hands.

It is not necessary to lay on hands when prophesying, but the two combined are powerful ways to impart and release blessings.

chapter thirteen

PROPHETIC PRESBYTERY

T HE APOSTLE PAUL makes mention of the prophetic presbytery, which must have been a standard function in the
early church. There is great need for local churches to have
prophetic presbyteries that will strengthen, release, and help the
church move into a greater level of breakthrough and ministry. I am
surprised by the number of churches that have never had a time for
prophetic presbytery, although this was practiced in the early church
and has been restored to the modern church for over fifty years.

> Neglect not the gift that is in thee, which was given thee
> by prophecy, with the laying on of the hands of the pres-
> bytery. Meditate upon these things; give thyself wholly to
> them; that thy profiting may appear to all.
> —1 TIMOTHY 4:14–15

Churches must have a revelation of the power of prophetic presbyteries and then set aside time for them periodically. David Blomgren's
book *Prophetic Gatherings in the Church* is a classic on the subject of

prophetic presbyteries. Unfortunately, it is now out of print. I will be referring to his book in this chapter.

WHAT IS PROPHETIC PRESBYTERY?

A prophetic presbytery is composed of presbyters, or elders, of a local church who are also apostles and prophets and who have the resident gift of prophecy. When a prophetic presbytery is held, these presbyters (elders) lay hands on and prophesy over selected believers to speak the will of God over them, impart gifts, and release them into their membership ministries. The presbyters do not have to be from the local church where the presbytery is being held. In other words, local churches can call in presbyters from other churches to conduct the presbytery.

A prophetic presbytery is composed of presbyters, or elders, of a local church who are also apostles and prophets and who have the resident gift of prophecy.

Bill Hamon defines *prophetic presbytery* as a time when two or more prophets or prophetic ministers lay hands on and prophesy over individuals at a specified time and place.[1] Prophetic presbyteries are conducted for several reasons:

1. For revealing a saint's membership ministry in the body of Christ

2. For ministering a prophetic rhema word of God to individuals

3. For the impartation and activation of divinely ordained gifts, graces, and callings

4. For revelation, clarification, and confirmation of leadership ministry in the local church

5. For the laying on of hands and prophecy over those who have been called and properly prepared to be an ordained minister serving in one of the fivefold gifts

A prophetic presbytery is different from receiving prophetic words from a prophetic team. Prophetic presbyteries are governmental because they are conducted by the authority (elders) of the church. Presbyteries are to deliver prophetic words to the people they have gathered to pray for, but prophetic presbyteries have more of a "setting and releasing" aspect for those receiving ministry. Candidates for receiving ministry are chosen by the leadership of the church. Prophetic presbytery is not a time for anyone and everyone to receive a word.

Presbytery team

The presbytery team can consist of two or more presbyters, although it is ideal to have three or four presbyters on the team. Each presbyter takes time to prophesy over the candidates before the entire congregation. Each presbyter has a portion of the word to release; no one presbyter will have the entire word of the Lord. Presbyters must work together as a team. There is no competition between the presbyters, particularly because they should all be mature (elders).

The presbytery is led by a senior presbyter (usually an apostle with the most experience and maturity among the presbyters). Apostles will be able to prophesy with authority and revelation from their apostolic office. They also have an anointing to set. Prophets, however, are much needed in a presbytery, because they bring detail and clarity by releasing the word of the Lord from the prophet's office. Apostles and prophets make a powerful team in a presbytery.

Presbyters with a resident gift of prophecy can prophesy on a regular basis to God's people. They do not have to wait for a special anointing to prophesy; they can prophesy because of the resident gift of prophecy. The simple gift of prophecy is for edification, exhortation, and comfort, but apostles and prophets can go beyond these and speak direction, correction, and revelation. They can do this because of other gifts, such as the word of wisdom, the word of knowledge, and faith, which operate through their offices. Therefore, a prophetic presbytery will go beyond edification, exhortation, and comfort. It will include impartation, direction, confirmation, and revelation because of the combination of the resident gift of prophecy in the presbyters and the strength and anointing of their offices.

The strength of a particular prophetic presbytery will depend upon the presbyters and candidates. The more mature and gifted the presbyters are, and the more qualified the candidates are, the stronger the prophetic flow will be. The strength of the presbytery, in part created through prayer, fasting, and worship, will be determined by the faith of the church and the spiritual atmosphere.

Strong utterances and impartations should be expected if a presbytery is conducted properly. God desires for churches to have strong prophetic gatherings. These should be times of great refreshing and blessing for the entire church. Even those not receiving ministry can rejoice and be blessed as they watch and listen while others in the body receive so much from the Lord. It is always the case that when others in the body are strengthened and released, the entire church is blessed.

Who should attend?

The entire leadership of the church should be present during a presbytery. They need to hear the prophetic words spoken over people who are under their leadership. The leadership of a church is responsible to oversee the members and has a responsibility to help guide the candidates after they receive prophetic ministry. Members should also be encouraged to come and give their support. The corporate anointing helps to enable a strong presbytery to take place. Those who are not receiving ministry should not sit idly by as mere spectators of what is transpiring. They should help create an atmosphere, through their faith and prayer, that will assist the presbyters and candidates to receive the full blessing of the Lord.

It is wise to invite presbyters who are new to the church and not too familiar with the people receiving ministry. It is also good to have a presbyter return, who has functioned as a presbyter before (if this is not the first presbytery). There may be leaders within the local church who can function on a presbytery, but it is recommended that the leadership bring in presbyters from outside the local church who are not familiar with the candidates.

Candidates for receiving ministry are chosen by the leadership of the church. Prophetic presbytery is not a time for anyone and everyone to receive a word.

After each presbyter has prophesied (although it is not necessary for all the presbyters to prophesy over each candidate), it is time for the presbytery to lay hands on and pray over the candidate (or candidates, if a couple). This is a time of impartation and the transfer of gifts and anointing. The candidate will be encouraged, confirmed, strengthened, and released into a greater sphere of ministry as a result of prophetic presbytery. The church will also be blessed by hearing the prophetic word that was spoken over the candidates. This will help the church and leadership to discern the gifting and calling upon the candidates. The church will be built up because key people (candidates) have received prophetic presbytery.

Candidates

Candidates should be members of the local church who have been selected by its leadership. They should be saved and Spirit filled, and they should evidence spiritual maturity. It is recommended that the candidates be members of a local church for at least a year to prevent people from joining a church just to receive this kind of ministry. Prophetic presbytery is not a time to fix problems that believers may have. It is unfair to the presbyters to select people who are not qualified to receive the specific kind of ministry that they have to offer.

While all believers can receive prophecy and churches today are raising up prophetic teams to accomplish this, prophetic presbytery is a time during which only a select few receive in-depth prophetic ministry. It is recommended that the number be limited to between three and seven settings. After candidates receive prophetic presbytery, time can be given to call people from the congregation and prophesy over them. This is to encourage believers, but it is not the main reason why the presbyters have come. The church can also receive corporate words during a time of prophetic presbytery.

Believers of a local church can request to be candidates for prophetic presbytery. However, the leadership bears the responsibility of selecting the candidates. Those who are chosen should be told beforehand in order to prepare spiritually for the prophetic presbytery. Fasting on the part of the candidates and the presbyters will always enhance the strength and accuracy of the prophetic word. The whole church can be encouraged to fast prior to a presbytery. This will create an atmosphere for the Holy Spirit to speak to the church.

That being said, it should also be made clear that people who do not desire prophetic presbytery should not be forced to receive it.

If a husband or wife desires to become a candidate for prophetic presbytery but his or her mate does not, this does not represent a disqualification. However, if one mate is not as qualified as the other and yet both desire ministry, it is advisable for them still to receive ministry as a couple (provided that both are saved). If a mate is unsaved, the believing mate can still receive ministry from the presbytery alone.

Candidates should be people whom the leadership of the church feels are about to enter into a new level of ministry. They can be potential leaders or potential ministers of the church. Large churches will have an abundance of candidates, and they must be chosen carefully and prayerfully. There may be a tendency for some people to feel overlooked, but the time frame must be understood by all, and no one should take offense if they are not chosen.

Location and duration

The presbytery should occur in the local church setting. It should not be done in a cell group or home meeting. The entire church should understand the importance of this time and participate if possible. A short message can be given before a presbytery, and worship should be done at intervals to keep the prophetic spirit strong. All prophecies should be recorded and later reviewed by the leadership. The candidate has the responsibility to take heed to the word spoken.

The presbytery can take place over several days. It takes time to minister in prophetic presbytery. This is not a time to call in prophets to prophesy over everything moving in your church.

A church can have a presbytery yearly or biyearly depending on the need. Leaders should spend time teaching and preparing the church if they have never had a presbytery. The church needs to have revelation and understand the importance of such a time.

RESTORATION OF THE PROPHETIC PRESBYTERY

The practice of the ministry of prophetic presbyteries remained absent from the church for many generations after the early church was dispersed until the Latter Rain Movement of the 1940s in North America. Many churches began to operate in presbyteries during the Latter Rain Movement. However, after a short time, the practice again declined significantly. One of the reasons for this is that very few books were written by leaders of the Latter Rain Movement.

We are living in times of restoration. Prophetic presbytery is a part of restoration truth that churches should receive and operate in. Restoration churches are recovering truth, revelation, and ministry that have been absent or neglected in the church for generations. With restored truth comes a greater ability for breakthrough and release of ministry.

Prophetic presbytery is like a "spiritual technology" that the enemy desires to keep from the local church because it can be so effective in strengthening the church. I have a heart to see it restored fully. I have seen firsthand the benefits of prophetic presbytery in Crusaders Church, over which I am the apostolic overseer.

Benefits of prophecy in a presbytery

David Blomgren mentions nine benefits of prophecy in a presbytery as follows:

1. Edification (1 Cor. 14:3)

2. Exhortation (1 Cor. 14:3)

3. Comfort (1 Cor. 14:3)

4. Direction (Acts 13:1–2)

5. Conferral (1 Tim. 4:14)

6. Confirmation (Acts 15:32)

7. Correction (1 Cor. 14:31; "learn" means corrective learning)

8. Judgment (Hos. 6:5)

9. Equipping of the saints (Eph. 4:11–12)[2]

Prophetic presbytery releases great grace to the hearers. The prophetic word is able to build us up and release our inheritances unto us.

> And now, brethren, I commend you to God, and to the word of his grace, which is able to build you up, and to give you an inheritance among all them which are sanctified.
>
> —ACTS 20:32

Believers need grace in order to serve God. Believers need an abundance of grace so they can "reign in life" (Rom. 5:17). One sign of an abundance of grace is an abundance of gifts (1 Cor. 1:4–7), and both gifts and grace are imparted during a prophetic presbytery.

The prophetic word is more than information. The prophetic word releases life (breath). Remember the experience of the prophet Ezekiel:

> So I prophesied as he commanded me, and the breath came into them, and they lived, and stood up upon their feet, an exceeding great army.
>
> —EZEKIEL 37:10

Prophetic presbytery is a time in which life is breathed into the recipient. The gifts and destiny of the candidate are revealed and activated. It causes believers to rise up and stand on their own feet. It is a key to raising up a strong army of believers.

We are living in times of restoration. Prophetic presbytery is a part of restoration truth that churches should receive and operate in.

Leaders are changed when they come into contact with the company of the prophets. Saul was released as the first king of Israel through the prophetic anointing:

> And it shall come to pass, when thou art come thither to the city, that thou shalt meet a company of prophets...and they shall prophesy: and the Spirit of the LORD will come upon thee, and thou shalt prophesy with them, and shalt be turned into another man.
>
> —1 SAMUEL 10:5–6

Prophetic presbytery is a time to release potential leaders into their callings and ministries. The strength of prophetic presbytery is the joining together of the anointings of the team. The team members strengthen and stir up one another as they minister together.

Prophetic presbytery is a time for learning the will of God and being comforted. It is a time to allow the prophets to speak. The presbyters minister as a team:

> Let the prophets speak two or three, and let the other judge. If any thing be revealed to another that sitteth by, let the first hold his peace. For ye may all prophesy one by one, that all may learn, and all may be comforted.
>
> —1 CORINTHIANS 14:29–31

As one ministers, others can receive revelation concerning the candidates. In this way, the candidates benefit from the ministry of several prophets.

As I mentioned above, I believe that prophetic presbytery is a spiritual technology from God that is designed to help leaders build strong churches. This is a day of restoration. Churches must appropriate all the benefits that God's gifts bring to the church.

I believe that as churches around the world take advantage of prophetic presbytery, they will move into apostolic strength and power.

Empowering through the laying on of hands

The Hebrew word for *lay* is *samach*, and the word for *laying on of hands* for an ordination or a sacrifice is *semicha*. The Greek word for *laying on of hands* is *epitithemi*. This word implies contact, which is a channel for transmission. Prophecy is a channel through which grace and gifts are transferred. The person receiving has the responsibility and obligation to steward the gifts and grace received. Timothy received a gift through prophecy with the laying on of hands of the presbytery.

> This charge I commit unto thee, son Timothy, according to the prophecies which went before on thee, that thou by them mightest war a good warfare.
> —1 TIMOTHY 1:18

The prophecies Timothy received helped him to war a good warfare. Paul reminded (charged) him according to these prophecies. Prophetic presbytery is not to be taken lightly by the recipient. Unto whom much is given, much is also required. The recipient has the responsibility and obligation to war with the prophetic word.

Prophetic words recorded during a presbytery should be meditated upon and used by the candidate as a weapon against the enemy.

David Blomgren mentions thirteen benefits of the laying on of hands and prophecy by the presbytery:

1. A greater realization of each one's responsibility to function in a ministry

2. A greater appreciation for the various ministries in the body of Christ and the need for them

3. A "setting in" of ministries in the local assembly

4. Finding one's place in the body of Christ

5. The confirmation of the will of God for the candidate

6. The further development of ministries within the local body

7. Specialized assistance through prophetic revelation and individual lives

8. The strengthening of the whole church in a better understanding of God's ways through receiving prophetic ministry

9. The raising of the spiritual level of the whole church through seeking the Lord in fasting and prayer

10. The receiving of prophetic direction for the whole church

11. The imparting of gifts and blessings to believers by the laying on of hands

12. A greater recognition of God's order in the authority of the local leadership as overseers of the lives of the people

13. A deposit of faith in the hearts of the congregation to see God's purposes fulfilled[3]

Prophetic gatherings are times when destinies are revealed and released. Prophecy has always been a vehicle through which the Lord has given direction, blessing, activation, and impartation to His people. This can be seen when Jacob gathered his sons together. Jacob spoke prophetically to his sons and detailed their destinies and inheritance:

> And Jacob called unto his sons, and said, Gather your-selves together, that I may tell you that which shall befall you in the last days. Gather yourselves together, and hear, ye sons of Jacob; and hearken unto Israel your father.
> —GENESIS 49:1–2

It is important for churches and believers to set aside times for prophetic gatherings. These can be times of power and release when accompanied by prayer and fasting and with the laying on of hands, which is one of the principle doctrines of the church (Heb. 6:1–2).

Sometimes the prophetic word spoken during a time of presbytery will not be fully fulfilled until years later. With prophetic presbytery, believers can prepare for the future by aligning themselves with the Word of the Lord. The Word of the Lord will be tested, but a believer walking in faith and fulfillment will see the desired result.

Moses prophesied over the tribes of Israel. The Word of God calls it a blessing:

> And this is the blessing, wherewith Moses the man of God blessed the children of Israel before his death.
> —DEUTERONOMY 33:1

Prophetic presbytery is a time of blessing. *Blessing* is the Hebrew word *berakah*, meaning a benediction. Moses was a prophet. Prophets have the grace, authority, and ability to release tremendous blessings. This is why presbyteries should consist of prophets who have the office of prophet as opposed to people with the gift of prophecy. Prophets have more grace and authority to release and bless people concerning their destinies.

Leaders must understand that the purpose of the fivefold ministry is for the perfecting of the saints. This includes preaching, teaching, training, activation, laying on of hands, and prophetic ministry. Believers cannot advance beyond their leadership, but a lack of quality prophetic ministry can be the difference between success and failure.

Presbytery meetings are not the only way for a believer to discern and understand the will of God. Each local church is responsible for the development and release of its members, but every believer is responsible to pray, study, and seek the will of God for himself or herself. Prophetic presbytery is not for lazy believers who desire a "shortcut" to understanding God's will. However, it is a tremendous benefit for believers. Prophetic presbytery is a ministry given by God's grace to help us walk in God's will for our lives.

chapter fourteen

DRAWING FROM
THE ANOINTING

I AM FINDING OUT that God is always ready. I know there are seasons and times and different moves of God, but I also know there are many people who have always spoken before their time. An example of this would be Bishop Charles Mason, founder of the Church of God in Christ.

Bishop Mason flowed in some heavy things. He was so many years ahead of the Church of God in Christ. He was singing in tongues and singing in the Spirit before miracles occurred, while most people had not gone beyond clapping and dancing. Smith Wigglesworth raised people from the dead. These men always seemed out of place. They would always get into the flow of something before others did.

It is good to have the move of God come into a city. It is good to have the timing of God when the Spirit of God says it is time to move and it suits the whole body of Christ.

However, when you press in to the prophetic move of God, when you stir that up, when you flow, God is not going to withhold something from you just because others are not ready to accept it.

The Bible says if you ask, it shall be given unto you. If you seek, you shall find. If you knock, the doors are going to open. God is not going to have you asking, seeking, and knocking and then say, "Well, I'm sorry. I can't open the door right now because it's just not time for that."

God will say, "Fine, you want it; I will give it to you even though I am not going to release this thing upon the whole body of Christ until maybe twenty years from now." God will drop that anointing on you, and you will be a church or a people ahead of your time. Then, years down the road, the whole body of Christ will come into it; they will all get the revelation. They can wait for that time if they want to, but I am not going to wait for it, because I am convinced that before Jesus Christ comes back, we are going to be flowing in the prophetic. The whole body of Christ will be flowing in miracles and deliverance because He is coming back for a glorious church. It is going to take a move of God, but He is able!

If there is a demand for the prophetic, if there is a hunger for miracles, I am going to tap in to that anointing and flow in it now, even though it may not seem like the proper season for it.

The Spirit of God has given me the revelation that you can flow in things ahead of your time. When Jesus's mother told Him there was no more wine at the wedding, He prophetically told her that His hour had not yet come (John 2:4). In other words, "It's not the time for this." Yet, He still performed the miracle.

If there is a demand for the prophetic, if there is a hunger for miracles,
I am going to tap in to that anointing and flow in it now.

There is always a group of people ahead of their time. Take, for instance, the Wright brothers. They were flying airplanes ahead of their time. Everyone thought they were crazy. Now we are flying all over the world. People probably said, "They are crazy. Look at poor Wilbur and Orville." That is what people will say when you get ahead of your time in the Spirit.

The rest of the people always catch up with the move of God after about ten years have passed. For example, in the church, God already moved people to get into the Word. We got into teaching. We were "Word churches." But there are still some churches that are not in the Word. That wave has passed them. They are still on the beach with their surfboards, looking for the wave.

What I am saying is that when the wave comes, you better jump and ride it! Do it then—or do it early. Where prophetic culture is concerned, stir it up, even if nobody else wants to. Maybe you can break it open for the rest of your local body of Christ.

TOUCHING THE MANTLE

One very important way to make sure you are part of God's flow and not an idle bystander is to get to where the anointing is. Like the woman with the issue of blood, touch the mantle of one who carries the anointing you need:

> For she said within herself, If I may but touch his garment,
> I shall be whole.
>
> —MATTHEW 9:21

The Rotherham translation says, "If only I touch his mantle."[1] The mantle represents the *anointing*. As we have noted earlier, Elisha received the anointing of Elijah both when Elijah called him by casting his mantle on him (1 Kings 19:19) and when Elijah was taken up by the heavenly chariot, dropping his mantle for Elisha to pick up (2 Kings 2:13). This represented the anointing coming upon him to stand in the office of a prophet. We call this the *prophetic mantle.*

Jesus walked and ministered as a prophet of God. He ministered under a prophetic mantle. This mantle also included healing and miracles. The woman with the issue of blood pressed through the crowd to touch His mantle. She was putting a demand upon His prophetic mantle. As a result, she received a miracle.

Different spiritual mantles have been given to different people. As you touch the mantle of a particular office, you will draw virtue and power from that anointing. You don't always have to touch a person physically; you can draw from them *spiritually* whether or not physical touch is involved.

Faith is the channel through which you draw the anointing. It is the pipeline.

Keep begging

> And when the men of that place had knowledge of him, they sent out into all that country round about, and brought unto him all that were diseased; and *besought* him that they might only touch the hem of his garment: and as many as touched were made perfectly whole.
> —MATTHEW 14:35–36, emphasis added

One translation says they "kept begging him." Have you ever had someone continue to beg you? They are demanding something of you. This is how you put a demand on the anointing.

According to Webster, to *beseech* means to beg for urgently or anxiously, to request earnestly, to implore, to make supplication. It means to seek. It is the laying aside of pride. You admit you have a need and beseech someone who has the ability to help you. Unless you recognize your need for and utter dependence upon the anointing, you will never put a demand on it.

> And whithersoever he entered, into villages, or cities, or country, they laid the sick in the streets, and *besought* him that they might touch if it were but the border of his garment: and as many as touched him were made whole.
>
> —MARK 6:56, emphasis added

Everywhere Jesus went, people were putting a demand on the anointing. They besought Him to touch His garment. They drew the healing and miracles out of Him. You may say, "This happened in every city because it was a sovereign move of God." You may think the people had nothing to do with it. But remember, it didn't happen in His hometown of Nazareth. They did not beseech to touch Him in Nazareth. These miracles didn't occur in Nazareth because the people didn't put a demand on the anointing. In other villages and cities, they did, and they were made whole.

As you touch the mantle of a particular office, you will draw virtue and power from that anointing.

Jesus always responded to people who put a demand on Him through their hunger for the things of God. He never turned them away empty. The spiritual principle here is what I call the law of supply and demand. Where there is no demand, there is no supply.

Apathetic, passive Christians don't receive much from the gifts of God.

Creating a demand

People came to hear Jesus because He created a demand by setting people free. (See, for example, Mark 1:26–34.) When people hear of miracles, they will gather to hear the word of God. They will come with expectancy and faith and draw from the anointing of the servant of God.

There is no substitute for miracles. They will cause a hunger to come into the hearts of people. Hungry hearts will always gather and put a demand on the anointing. Unbelievers will not put a demand on the anointing, but believers will.

If we want hungry people, we must have miracles. Some churches wonder why their people are so unconcerned and apathetic about serving God. People drag themselves to services. Some pastors will try all kinds of programs to raise the excitement of the people, but there is no substitute for doing it God's way. Where there are miracles, the people will gather willingly. Their faith level will rise, and they will put a demand on the anointing for more.

> And straightway many were gathered together, insomuch that there was no room to receive them, no, not so much as about the door: and he preached the word unto them.
> —MARK 2:2

Some only show up because the pastor tells them to or because they are just in the habit of going to church. Then miracles, prophecies, and healing will not flow out of the servant of God to the extent that they will where there is a demand. Of course a minister can stir up the gifts of God and minister by faith. However, when the faith of the *people* is high, it is much easier to minister. Jesus could, in His own hometown, do no mighty work because of their unbelief. Unbelief always hinders the flow of the anointing. Faith releases the flow.

FAITH PUTS A DEMAND ON THE ANOINTING

Faith releases the anointing. Unbelief blocks the anointing. The woman with the issue of blood put a demand on the anointing with her faith:

> And Jesus, immediately knowing in himself that virtue had gone out of him, turned him about in the press, and said, Who touched my clothes?
> —MARK 5:30

> And he said unto her, Daughter, thy faith hath made thee whole; go in peace, and be whole of thy plague.
> —MARK 5:34

Faith is like a vacuum that draws the anointing. Jesus not only ministered with the anointing, but He also let the people know He was anointed (Luke 4:18). When they heard He was anointed, it was their responsibility to believe and receive from His anointing. The people of Nazareth did not believe and could not draw from His anointing. He could do no mighty work in Nazareth because of their unbelief. If they would have believed, they could have drawn from His anointing.

Faith comes by hearing (Rom. 10:17). That is why we need to *hear* about the anointing. We need teaching concerning the anointing.

What is the anointing?

The words *unction* and *anointing* here are taken from the same Greek word *charisma*. *Charisma* means an unguent or smearing (represented by smearing with oil). It also means an endowment of the Holy Spirit. An endowment is a gift of the Holy Spirit. It is the power or ability of God. There are diversities of gifts (endowments or miraculous faculties).

> But ye have an unction from the Holy One, and ye know all things.
>
> —1 JOHN 2:20

> But the anointing which ye have received of him abideth in you.
>
> —1 JOHN 2:27

To draw from the anointing is to receive from the gift or ability of God. You can receive healing, deliverance, and miracles in this way. Apostles, prophets, evangelists, pastors, and teachers have an anointing given to them from God. They have endowments or miraculous faculties given to them by grace. These endowments are given for the benefit of the saints. We must put a demand on these gifts and endowments.

> And Jesus said, Somebody hath touched me: for I perceive that virtue is gone out of me.
>
> —LUKE 8:46

Jesus perceived that "virtue" had left Him. The woman with the issue of blood drew virtue out of Him with her faith. As I mentioned in chapter 12, the word *virtue* is the Greek word *dunamis*, which means power, ability, strength, or might. When you put a demand on the anointing, you draw out the power of God. Power is released on your behalf. Thus, the anointing is the virtue or power of God.

> When she had heard of Jesus, came in the press behind, and touched his garment.
>
> —MARK 5:27

This woman had heard of Jesus. She had heard about the healing anointing that was upon Him. She had heard that a prophet of God was ministering in Israel.

Unbelievers will not put a demand on the anointing, but believers will.

When people hear about the anointing, their faith will increase in this area, and they will then have the knowledge and faith to put a demand on the anointing. We need to know about the apostle's anointing, the prophet's anointing, and the teacher's anointing. We need to know about the healing anointing and the miracle anointing. We need to know about special anointings given by the Holy Spirit.

The more people hear and are taught about the anointing, the greater will be their capacity to put a demand on it. As a pastor of a local church, I teach the members about different gifts and anointings. This builds their faith in that area. When ministers come to minister at our church, I tell the members about the anointing on the person's life. They then have the responsibility to draw from and put a demand on that anointing by their faith.

We cannot be passive and expect to receive from these gifts. We must be active with our faith. Passive, apathetic saints do not receive from the anointing. I have ministered in places where I had to spend the first several nights getting the people to *activate* their faith. Then they could put a demand on the anointing in my life. People have to have a hunger and thirst for the things of the Spirit. Hungry souls will always draw from the anointing.

> And it came to pass, that the father of Publius lay sick of a fever and of a bloody flux: to whom Paul entered in, and prayed, and laid his hands on him, and healed him.

So when this was done, others also, which had diseases in the island, came, and were healed:

Who also honoured us with many honours; and when we departed, they laded us with such things as were necessary.

—ACTS 28:8–10

After the father of Publius was healed, the whole island of Melita came to be healed. They put a demand on the anointing in Paul's life. Notice that they honored Paul with many honors. Honoring the servant of God is a key to receiving from the anointing in his or her life. The scripture states that the people came. They came with the sick, expecting to be healed. They put action to their faith, and they came. You will find that most of the people who received miracles from Jesus either came or were brought to Him. Many besought Him.

Many in this country wonder why miracles occur so much in foreign countries. Many of the ones who attend crusades walk for miles to come to a meeting. Some travel for days. That is putting a demand on the anointing. Healing and miracles happen as a result. In America, many believers will not travel two blocks—and wonder why they don't receive miracles.

And believers were the more added to the Lord, multitudes both of men and women.

Insomuch that they brought forth the sick into the streets, and laid them on beds and couches, that at the least the shadow of Peter passing by might overshadow some of them.

There came also a multitude out of the cities round about unto Jerusalem, bringing sick folks, and them which were vexed with unclean spirits: and they were healed every one.

—ACTS 5:14–16

Here we see people coming "out of the cities round about unto Jerusalem." Where there is a demand, there is a supply. There was enough anointing available to heal *everyone*. These people put a demand on the anointing that flowed from the apostles. When people come to meetings, sometimes from long distances, and put a demand on the gift, they will receive miracles.

And it came to pass on a certain day, as he was teaching, that there were Pharisees and doctors of the law sitting by, which were come out of every town of Galilee, and Judaea, and Jerusalem: and the *power* of the Lord was present to heal them.

—LUKE 5:17, emphasis added

The word *power* here is also *dunamis* (again, the same word translated as "virtue" in Luke 8:46). The woman with the issue of blood drew virtue from the body of Jesus with her faith. So we can say that healing virtue was in the house as Jesus taught. When healing virtue (anointing) is present, we can use our faith to put a demand on that anointing. It will then be released for healing.

And, behold, men brought in a bed a man which was taken with a palsy: and they sought means to bring him in, and to lay him before him.

And when they could not find by what way they might bring him in because of the multitude, they went upon the housetop, and let him down through the tiling with his couch into the midst before Jesus.

> And when he saw their faith, he said unto him, Man,
> thy sins are forgiven thee.
>
> —LUKE 5:18–20

They put a demand on the anointing present in that room through their faith. As a result, healing virtue was released, and the man was healed of palsy. There are times when the presence of the Lord is thick like a cloud in a service. When the anointing is present to this degree, all we need to do is use our faith to put a demand upon it. Healing and miracles come as a result of putting a demand on the anointing.

We cannot be passive and expect to receive from these gifts.
We must be active with our faith.

We put a demand on the anointing with our *faith*. The Lord has given us the gift of faith for this purpose. The Lord desires that we use our faith to put a demand (withdrawal) on the gifts of God. Many never use their faith for this purpose.

Congregations that are built up in faith will have a tool they can use to receive from the gifts of God. Faith is a channel through which the anointing flows. Faith is like a light switch that starts the electricity flow. It is like the starter on a car, which ignites the power that turns the engine. Faith is the spark that ignites the explosive power of God. It ignites the power gifts of faith, healing, and miracles.

Faith ignites the revelation gifts of word of wisdom, word of knowledge, and discerning of spirits. It ignites the utterance gifts of tongues, interpretation, and prophecy. Faith releases the ministry gifts of apostles, prophets, evangelists, pastors, and teachers.

Faith comes by hearing. The more people hear about the gifts of God, the more faith they will receive to draw from them. As a pastor, I teach on different operations and administrations of the Spirit. I release people with different anointings and administrations to minister to the people. I teach people concerning these gifts and release them to use their faith to put a demand on these gifts.

It is amazing how profoundly ministers are able to minister in the atmosphere that is created through teaching and releasing. The people use their faith to pull the anointing right out of them, and the flow becomes so great, we have to purposely shut it off until the next service.

How to Put a Demand on the Anointing

The woman with the issue of blood put a demand on the healing anointing and received her miracle. Too often God's people do not receive miracles and healing because they do not place a demand on the anointing. The anointing upon and within ministry gifts is a supply. We must learn how to put a demand upon that supply and draw from it.

There is available to every believer a supply of the Spirit. A supply is a storehouse or a reservoir. When I look at ministry gifts, I see a person who is a living reservoir. In that reservoir is a supply of the anointing. It is my responsibility to draw from that supply. Men and women of God have miracles, revelation, and deliverance for you in that reservoir. If you put a demand on the anointing in that reservoir, miracles will flow out of them to you. Utterances will flow out of them into you.

Virtue came out of Jesus because the people drew from His anointing:

And the whole multitude sought to touch him: for there went virtue out of him, and healed them all.

—LUKE 6:19

SUPPLY AND DEMAND

The Lord spoke to my heart the fact that there is always a supply when there is a demand. The drug problems in our cities would not exist if there was no demand for drugs. Because there is a demand for drugs, there is a supply. It is the same with the anointing. If there is no demand, there will be no supply. Hungry saints who put a demand on ministry gifts will always have a supply of the anointing. I have ministered in churches where there was such a hunger and thirst for the anointing until they literally pulled the power right out of me. I have ministered in other places where there was no demand, and as a result, nothing happened. The people just sat back and waited for something to happen, and nothing did. There was no hunger or expectancy for revelation, utterances, or miracles.

These people were putting a demand on the anointing. They drew it out by seeking to touch Him. You can literally pull the anointing out of ministry gifts by your faith. If these people had just sat back and waited for Jesus to put it on them, they probably would not have received anything. Many times believers just sit back and wait for the man or woman of God to do something. All the while God is waiting for *us* to do something. He has placed the supply in our midst, and it is up to us to draw from it.

Because I teach the members of our local assembly to draw from the ministry gifts that minister in our services, telling them to put a demand on the anointing of the apostles, prophets, evangelists, pastors, and teachers, they receive the anointing. I teach them that these gifts from God have a supply in them, and it is their responsibility to draw from that supply.

Many ministers who have ministered at our local church are shocked by the high level of anointing they have been able to flow in. This has happened because I have taught the people to pull it out of them. Ministers love to minister in that type of atmosphere. The flow is much easier because the people are pulling *from* you instead of blocking you.

When Jesus was passing by the two blind men, they had to make some noise and draw Jesus's attention. They also drew the disapproving attention of the crowd. But who got the miracle? It was not the ones who tried to stop the men from crying out:

> And, behold, two blind men sitting by the way side, when they heard that Jesus passed by, cried out, saying, Have mercy on us, O Lord, thou son of David.
> And the multitude rebuked them, because they should hold their peace: but they cried the more, saying, Have mercy on us, O Lord, thou son of David.
> —MATTHEW 20:30–31

These men put a *demand* on Jesus. They cried out even when the multitude was rebuking them, telling them to be silent. They had to press past the opposition of the crowd to receive their miracle. If they had remained silent, they would not have received a miracle. They had to put a demand on the anointing. Jesus was passing by. If they did not put a demand on His anointing, He would have passed *them* by.

Faith is a channel through which the anointing flows.

It is like drawing money from a bank. You must go to the teller with a withdrawal slip and make a demand on the account. If you never make a demand on the account, you will never withdraw anything from the account.

Jesus was telling the people in His hometown of Nazareth that He was anointed:

> The Spirit of the Lord is upon me, because he hath anointed me to preach the gospel to the poor; he hath sent me to heal the brokenhearted, to preach deliverance to the captives, and recovering of sight to the blind, to set at liberty them that are bruised, to preach the acceptable year of the Lord.
>
> —LUKE 4:18–19

It was up to them to put a demand on His anointing. They could have drawn the gospel, the healing, and the deliverance right out of Him. They could have pulled the virtue and power out of Him. But they didn't. Their unbelief blocked the flow of the anointing. Instead of receiving miracles, they received nothing. Then Jesus said:

> A prophet is not without honour, but in his own country, and among his own kin, and in his own house.
> And he could there do no mighty work, save that he laid his hands upon a few sick folk, and healed them.
>
> —MARK 6:4–5

There, right in their midst, was supply—a reservoir of the anointing. In that reservoir was salvation, healing, deliverance, and miracles. Jesus was a walking reservoir of the anointing. They had the chance to put a demand on it and draw from it, but they did not because of unbelief. They did not see Him as a reservoir of the anointing but rather as a carpenter: "Is this not the carpenter, the son of Mary, the brother of James, and Joses, and of Juda, and Simon?" (Mark

6:3). They looked at Him and judged Him in the natural. However, if they had looked at Him in the Spirit, they would have seen Him as a reservoir or a pool of the anointing. They would have drawn out of Him miracles and healing by faith.

We need to learn from this. We must put a demand upon the anointing and draw the miracles out of Him. There is nothing wrong with ministers telling people what they are anointed for. If you have a healing anointing, tell the people. Give them a chance to draw from that anointing. If you have a prophetic anointing, tell the people. Let them draw the prophetic words out of you. If you have a teaching anointing, tell the people. Let them draw the knowledge, understanding, and revelation out of you.

Elisha had enough anointing *in his bones* to raise a man from the dead. Imagine the anointing that was available to Israel while he was alive! But because they did not put a demand on the anointing in his life, they did not receive the miracles they needed. Every leper in Israel needed a miracle. The Lord, in His mercy, saw the need and provided the man of God with His anointing. It was up to Israel to put a demand upon it. Their needs were not met because there was no demand. There was no faith. There was no honor. If they would have honored the prophet of God, they would have been healed. The anointing was available. It was strong enough. But there was no demand. Since there was no demand, there was no supply.

DRAWING FROM THE ANOINTING

There are other examples in Scripture of people putting a demand on the anointing:

> And he cometh to Bethsaida; and they bring a blind man unto him, and *besought* him to touch him.
> —MARK 8:22, emphasis added

And he arose out of the synagogue, and entered into Simon's house. And Simon's wife's mother was taken with a great fever; and they *besought* him for her.
—LUKE 4:38, emphasis added

And they bring unto him one that was deaf, and had an impediment in his speech; and they *beseech* him to put his hand upon him.
—MARK 7:32, emphasis added

And when they wanted wine, the mother of Jesus saith unto him, They have no wine.

Jesus saith unto her, Woman, what have I to do with thee? mine hour is not yet come.

His mother saith unto the servants, Whatsoever he saith unto you, do it.
—JOHN 2:3–5

In the last scripture, Mary drew the miracle out of Jesus by putting a demand on Him. She presented to Him a need and He responded, even though it was not His time to act.

This was the beginning of His miracle ministry. "This beginning of miracles did Jesus in Cana of Galilee…" (John 2:11). It all began because His mother presented to Him a need for wine. Often in ministry, I will begin to flow in prophecy, miracles, or healing because I sense a demand. People can present these needs to you in such a way that it will begin to cause a miracle flow to come out of you. It is like priming the pump. Once the water begins to flow, it comes gushing out.

Jesus said that out of our bellies would flow rivers of living water. All we need to do is get the flow started. It will begin when there is a demand. Once it begins, it will continue to flow until every need is met.

Draw from anointed vessels

The story of the first miracle of Jesus at Cana of Galilee is prophetic. (See John 2:6–10.) The six water pots of stone represent the earthen vessels that the Lord uses. (See 2 Corinthians 4:7.) Six is the number of man. Man was created on the sixth day. Jesus commanded that the vessels be filled with water. Water represents the Word (Eph. 5:26). Servants of God need to be filled with the Word of God. Apostles, prophets, evangelists, pastors, and teachers are to be filled with the Word. The Lord will fill you with the Word so that others can draw from you.

Jesus then told them to draw out of the vessels. As they drew out, the water was turned into wine. Wine represents the Holy Spirit. It represents the anointing of God. We are to draw out of the ministry gifts. *Draw* is the Greek word *antleo*, meaning to dip water with a bucket or pitcher.

We are to use our buckets and draw out of the earthen vessels that God has filled with His Word. When I get around anointed ministry gifts, my bucket is out and I am ready to draw. When the Lord's vessels come into the local church, we are to draw from them. We draw because we have needs. The mother of Jesus said to him, "They have no wine" (John 2:3). There was a need at the marriage feast for wine. When there is a need for the anointing and flow of the Spirit, we must draw out of the earthen vessels the Lord has given us. We must use our faith to draw out the wine when there is a need.

Prophets must spend time filling up on the Word. Allow the Lord to fill your vessel up with the water of the Word. As you minister, allow the saints of God to draw from you. There are so many with needs. People need the wine of the Holy Ghost that will flow from us.

Truly, whether filling up or drawing from the Holy Ghost, we need the power of God flowing in our lives. It is my sincere hope and prayer that the revelation shared in this book will tremendously bless God's people to begin to receive in abundance the fullness of all of the gifts of God in the body of Christ, especially the all-important prophetic gift.

Appendix A

PROPHETIC EXERCISES TO DEVELOP BELIEVERS

THE FOLLOWING EXERCISES are used in our local assembly to help develop believers in their ability to exercise the prophetic gift. They have been instrumental in releasing thousands of believers to prophesy and in increasing the level of the prophetic flow in our congregation. I offer these exercises for use in a local church setting under qualified leadership.

Around the circle

This exercise is best used as a "warm-up" activation. The team leader selects a minister who will prophesy to the circle member directly to his left or right. After the first minister has finished, then the circle member who just received ministry begins to prophesy to the circle member on his other side. This chainlike ministry continues all the way around the circle.

All on one

Everyone in the circle takes a turn ministering to a single circle member. The result will be in-depth ministry to the single recipient. As a result, the ministry recipient will be "jump-started" into flowing with the spirit of prophecy. This exercise will also demonstrate the flow of a prophetic presbytery.

One on all

This exercise is designed to "stretch" a minister past his or her usual limitations. The minister is required to prophesy to everyone in the circle. This exercise also builds confidence and faith that God will reveal His word.

One prophetic word

A minister is required to give a single prophetic word to everyone in his circle. Each circle member ministers in this way. Circle members are to write down only the words that were directly given to them by others. After everyone in the circle has ministered, each circle member is to read each of the words that were spoken over him or her and prophesy what the Lord is saying to him through all the words put together. This exercise enables the ministers to discern a common flow and to build spiritual concentration and interpretation.

Switch/change

This method can be applied with any of the activation exercises. At the command of the team leader, the minister will switch, or the recipients will change. A fast change will help to develop accuracy in the ministers. A slow change will enable more in-depth personal ministry to manifest from the minister. The spontaneous switching of ministers will exercise the ministers' ability to hold a prophetic word and their ability to be ready to minister at a moment's notice.

In order to keep a smooth flow, team leader's can indicate a switch by saying, "Switch," and pointing to the next minister.

See a picture

This exercise will activate prophetic visions. The minister will use his faith to receive a picture from God that pertains to the person he is ministering to. Once he receives the picture, the minister is then required to render a description of the picture through the prophetic word. This prophetic explanation should never add to or take away from the picture. It should contain only what is seen.

Write what you hear

This is an exercise in the ministry of the prophetic scribe. Circle members should be equipped with a pen and notepad. Circle members should pray to God, asking for divine instruction (imparted knowledge). Immediately after praying, everyone should begin to write what they hear. Writing down a lead such as "My daughter/son..." can help overcome writer's block. Team leaders may ask circle members to take turns reading out loud what God has given to them.

Group prophecy

A minister from the circle is chosen to give a common prophecy that pertains to all the circle members. This exercise is designed to help the minister become comfortable with ministering to whole groups of people such as a congregation.

Prophesy from a lead (a "diving board")

"Diving boards" are subjects that everyone has in common, for example, finances and family. The team leader will choose a topic for the minister. The minister then is directed to prophesy to a circle member concerning that topic. Using a lead helps to eliminate fear from the minister.

The blind prophet

A minister from the circle prophesies to someone whom they did not choose and cannot see. Typically, the team leader places a blindfold over the eyes of the minister and then selects someone to stand behind the minister. The minister is instructed to prophesy to the person standing behind him or her. This exercise builds faith in God. It results in a more accurate and deeper prophetic flow.

Sing a prophecy

This exercise is designed to activate a minister into the song of the Lord and the new song. The minister is required to sing the prophetic word. Through faith the minister will find that his spiritual ear is opened to melodies given by God. Sometimes these tunes never before have been heard.

Give a word of knowledge

This exercise will cause the minister to reveal detailed and personal information from God about the ministry recipient. To begin, the minister should pray for God to give him or her divine knowledge. Then the team leader will offer a lead that requires the minister to fill in the blanks. Examples of leads are, "When you were fifteen years old…," "You have asked Me…," "People have told you…," "There is someone here who has…," and so forth. Confirmation that this gift is operating will be that the minister, without prior knowledge about the revealed information, has spoken information that is true.

Impart your gift

This is an exercise in the "laying on of hands." The leader will select ministers who have a strong operating gift(s) from God. The ministers will then lay hands on selected circle members who desire or need an impartation of a gift. While laying on hands, the minister should pray and ask God to allow the gift to transfer. An immediate result will be a display of power that causes the recipient to react, such as falling down in the Spirit. The long-term results will be that the recipient begins to operate in the gift that he or she has received.

Popcorn

The team leader will select a minister and five circle members. The minister is required to prophesy to all of the five circle members in less than three minutes. Team leaders will stop the minister when the time is up. The time limit and the number of prophesy recipients may vary. This exercise helps eliminate timidity and thought interference. The word of the Lord will burst from the mouth of the minister, and a deeper flow will result.

Prophesy Scripture verses

Team leaders will be prepared with Scripture cards. The scriptures will cover various topics. A minister from the circle will select and silently read one or more cards. After returning the cards to the team leader, the minister will prophesy to a circle member according to each scripture. The minister's prophetic utterance should be similar to the wording of the scriptures. Accepted variations include using modern-day English, speaking in the first person, and addressing the words to "My daughter/son." If the scriptures selected are in line with the needs of the recipient, all will know that the minister was led by God. Once a prophetic flow has been established, this activation can continue without the use of prompt cards. Ministers will then be stretched into using parts of the Word that they have already studied. This exercise helps to ensure that the prophetic utterances are in line with the Word of God.

PROPHETIC PROTOCOL

1. Always prophesy in love. Love the people you minister to. Love is the motivation behind prophecy (1 Cor. 14:1). Do not prophesy out of bitterness, hurt, or anger. Love always seeks to edify. Love is not rude. Love is not harsh or condemning. Be sensitive to the person you are ministering to. Be polite.

2. Prophesy according to your proportion of faith (Rom. 12:6). Do not copy others. Be yourself. God wants us all to be originals, not copies. We lose our own God-given individuality and uniqueness when we copy others. Strive to do your best and to be yourself.

3. Avoid being too demonstrative, dramatic, theatrical, or showy when ministering prophetically.

4. When ministering to a person of the opposite sex, do not lay your hands on any area of the person's body that could be considered sensitive. If you must touch, lay your hands gently on the head or on the shoulder. You may ask another person of the same sex as the recipient to place a hand on the person for the purpose of impartation and healing.

5. Do not allow people to worship you! Stay humble when people give praise and good reports about the ministry they received from you. Remember to worship Jesus. The testimony of Jesus is the spirit of prophecy.

6. Don't be a prophetic "lone ranger." Learn to minister with others. We only know in part and prophesy in part. Submitting to others is a way to avoid pride. Prefer others when ministering. Do not be a prophetic "hog." Give others a chance to minister. Don't take up all the time. Learn to be a team player. A good follower makes a good leader.

7. Eliminate excessive hand motions, which distract the ministry recipient. This includes motions such as pointing, waving, and making fists. Also avoid rocking the person back and forth. Do not speak in tongues excessively while ministering prophetically. We can generally speak in tongues while beginning to get into the flow, but afterward stay with the known words of prophecy.

8. Never release a prophetic word that is contrary to the written Word of God. It is important for prophetic people to be students of the Word. Study to show yourself approved.

9. Know your strengths and limitations. Some people are stronger in certain areas of the prophetic than others. Do not attempt to go beyond your measure of grace. We are not in a competition; we are not trying to outdo others.

10. Remember, the spirit of the prophet is subject to the prophet (1 Cor. 14:32). God does not give us something we cannot control. You should always have rule over your spirit (Prov. 25:28). Never allow things to get out of control.

11. Do not be repetitious while prophesying. This often happens when people speak too long. Stop when the Holy Spirit stops.

12. Use a recording device when possible. This will give the recipient the ability to write the prophecy down and review it. This avoids allowing the recipient to report that the minister said something he or she did not say, and it makes it possible for the prophecy to be judged by the leadership.

13. Speak in the first person. This may take time and practice to get accustomed to, but you are the voice of the Lord on the earth. This will result in a deeper flow prophetically.

NOTES

CHAPTER 5
PROPHETS WHO PROTECT

1. Jim Goll and Lou Engle, *Elijah's Revolution* (Shippensburg, PA: Destiny Image, 2002), 99.

2. John Paul Jackson, *Unmasking the Jezebel Spirit* (North Sutton, NH: Streams Publications, 2002), 33.

CHAPTER 12
IMPARTATION THROUGH PROPHETIC MINISTRY

1. Richard Weymouth, *The Modern Speech New Testament* (New York: The Baker and Taylor Co., 1905), 352.

CHAPTER 13
PROPHETIC PRESBYTERY

1. Bill Hamon, *Prophets and Personal Prophecy* (Shippensburg, PA: Destiny Image, 1987).

2. David Blomgren, *Prophetic Gatherings in the Church* (Saugus, CA: Temple Publishing, 1979).

3. Ibid.

CHAPTER 14
DRAWING FROM THE ANOINTING

1. Joseph Rotherham, *Rotherham's Emphasized Bible* (Grand Rapids, MI: Kregel Classics, 1959).

Activate
the Ultimate
Power Source

978-1-59979-246-0 / $9.99

This book combines powerful prayers with decrees taken from Scripture to help you overcome demonic influence and opposition in your life.

Discover how to release the fire of the living God to:

- PREACH
- PROPHESY
- HEAL THE SICK
- CAST OUT DEMONS
- AND MORE!

ORDER THIS AMAZING
REFERENCE HANDBOOK FOR
DEFEATING THE DEVIL TODAY!

Charisma
HOUSE
A STRANG COMPANY

FREE NEWSLETTERS
TO HELP EMPOWER YOUR LIFE

Why subscribe today?

☐ **DELIVERED DIRECTLY TO YOU.** All you have to do is open your inbox and read.

☐ **EXCLUSIVE CONTENT.** We cover the news overlooked by the mainstream press.

☐ **STAY CURRENT.** Find the latest court rulings, revivals, and cultural trends.

☐ **UPDATE OTHERS.** Easy to forward to friends and family with the click of your mouse.

CHOOSE THE E-NEWSLETTER THAT INTERESTS YOU MOST:

- Christian news
- Daily devotionals
- Spiritual empowerment
- And much, much more

SIGN UP AT: **http://freenewsletters.charismamag.com**

8178